The Church Established

An Illustrated History of the Church

Created and Produced by Jaca Book

An outline by chapter can be found on the last two pages of this volume.

The Church Established

An Illustrated History of the Church

From 180 to 381

Translated and adapted by John Drury
Illustrated by Antonio Molino

 Winston Press   430 Oak Grove   Minneapolis, Minnesota 55403

Published in Italy under the title
L'epoca d'oro: La chiesa e la sua storia
Copyright © 1980 Jaca Book Edizioni

**Licensed publisher and distributor
of the English-language edition:**

Winston Press, Inc.
430 Oak Grove
Minneapolis, Minnesota 55403
United States of America

Agents:
Canada—
LeDroit/Novalis-Select
135 Nelson St.
Ottawa, Ontario
Canada   KIN   7R4

Australia, New Zealand, New Guinea, Fiji Islands—
Dove Communications, Pty. Ltd.
203 Darling Road
East Malvern, Victoria   3145
Australia

United Kingdom, Ireland, and South Africa—
Fowler-Wright Books, Ltd.
Burgess St.
Leominster, Herefordshire
England

Created and produced by Jaca Book, Milan
Color selection: Carlo Scotti, Milan
Printing: Grafiche Lithos Carugate, Milan
Binding: LEM Opera, Milan

Acknowledgments
The Scripture quotations in chapters 15 and 51 are taken from
Revised Standard Version Common Bible, copyright © 1973 by
the Division of Christian Education of the National Council
of the Churches of Christ in the U.S.A. Used by permission.

History Consultant: The Rev. Marvin R. O'Connell
Professor of History, University of Notre Dame

Winston Staff: Florence Flugaur, Meredith Montgomery—editorial
Chris Larson, Keith McCormick—design

Special Editorial Assistance (Chapters 8–15): Mary and Herb Montgomery

Library of Congress Catalog Card Number: 79–67831
ISBN: 0–03–056824–2

5 4 3 2 1

An Illustrated History of the Church

The Church Established

Introduction

In the time span described in *The Church Established*, the Christian community grew and flourished amid many difficulties.

Most outstanding in this era are the persecutions in which many Christians were martyred. One cause of the persecutions was the pagan ruling class's fear of Christianity. Pagans saw that the Christian life style and ideals attracted many converts, and they feared that eventually the Christian Church would force its values on the whole empire. Mostly because they did not understand these Christian values, pagan emperors decided to destroy the Church. The result was a series of terrible persecutions which came to a bloody climax under Diocletian in the years 303–311. The persecutions ended when the Church was tolerated, then favored under Emperor Constantine.

Now free from outside dangers, the Church faced a danger from within—the heresy of Arianism, a false belief that denied the divinity of Christ. The Church's fierce internal strife over Arianism almost brought about the destruction that the pagan emperors' violence had failed to accomplish. But the Church survived this struggle with heresy, a struggle that reminds us that in this world, the Church is always a pilgrim who must expect, in imitation of Jesus, both defeat and victory.

Marvin R. O'Connell

1. Around the year 200,
the Christian community
was beginning to look
like a large,
well-organized Church,
and the Christian message
was being spread
to those living
outside the Church.

Thanks to the work of missionaries, the Christian Church had spread rapidly through many parts of the Roman empire. Around the year 200 there were many converts to Christianity in the eastern part of the empire. At this time, a fairly large Christian community also lived in Rome, under the guidance of their bishop. The bishop of Rome, like other important bishops, was called *papa* meaning "father." From this came the word *pope*, a special name for the bishop of Rome.

Near the end of the second century, the Roman empire had many political and eco-

nomic problems. In this time of unrest, people yearned for truth and salvation. The old pagan religion of Rome and the ideas of philosophers no longer satisfied them. Christianity and other eastern religions offered hope and satisfaction.

The spread of Christianity was greatly helped by its new emphasis on love and community. Christians shared food, visited the sick, and helped each other in many other ways. Also, they organized schools and developed Christian art. They kept in touch with one another by writing letters and by sharing

written works about Christianity. In times of persecution, they faced death rather than give up their faith in Jesus.

Like pagan religious groups and the Jewish synagogue, Christians had local meeting places and they also had a community fund of money. Each Christian community was headed by a bishop, who was in charge of all matters relating to worship and the Christian faith. The bishop was greatly assisted by priests and deacons, and in time they came to be his chief helpers.

2. Outsiders were amazed at the friendship and harmony among Christians. At times, of course, Christians quarreled, but their faith in Jesus Christ helped them grow in love for each other.

The Christian faith spread fairly rapidly among all social classes and throughout the Roman empire. Outsiders were amazed by the closeness and unity of Christians. Christians shared a common faith, followed the teachings of their leaders, helped each other in difficulties, and came together for prayer and worship. Even though Christians had faults and sometimes argued with each other, their example of sharing and helping made a good impression on outsiders.

Many non-Christians were angered by the Christians' unity. They accused Christians of serious crimes without bothering to find out whether the accusations were really true. But some non-Christians wanted to find out more about the Christian way of life, and so they asked their Christian friends about it.

One such person was a man named Diognetus. In a letter which still exists today, a Christian friend tried to answer Diognetus's questions about Christianity.

Diognetus was particularly interested in Christian love and in the Christian attitude toward the world. His friend explained that a new thing about Christian love was that Jesus

commanded his followers to love all human beings and not to pass judgment on anyone. By contrast, pagans—even the best pagan philosophers—believed that friendship was a purely natural thing so that a person became friends only with those people who seemed worthy of receiving that friendship.

To explain the Christian attitude toward the world, Diognetus's Christian friend used a beautiful expression. He wrote: "Christians are in the world but not of the world." This meant that the commandment to love everyone prevented Christians from living for themselves alone. They could not lock out the world. They could not abandon other people who were less appealing, less intelligent, or even less good. Christians loved others because they loved God, who had first loved them. The friend ended the letter by saying that he would pray to the Lord for Diognetus, asking God to help Diognetus find the truth. He urged Diognetus to pray, too.

3. A Christian writer,
Minucius Felix, wrote
a famous book in the form
of a conversation
or dialogue
between two friends.
In this dialogue,
one man, a Christian,
explained and defended
Christian beliefs
to his pagan friend.

Minucius Felix was born in Africa around the year 200. He was well educated and became a lawyer in Rome. Minucius was convinced that humans could arrive at the truth about God by reasoning, even without the aid of Sacred Scripture. He believed that thinking people could realize that there could be only one God, not many gods as pagans believed. To defend this view and to give an accurate description of Christian living, Minucius composed a dialogue in Latin, entitled *Octavius*.

This dialogue presents a conversation between two friends traveling from Rome to nearby Ostia. Caecilius is a pagan; his friend, Octavius, is a Christian. Caecilius stops along the way to pay homage to the statue of a pagan god. Octavius gently teases him, and the two friends begin to talk about the true

nature of God. Caecilius says, "We are surrounded by mystery, and we are not capable of solving the puzzle. Since our minds are not strong enough, it is better to believe in the religion of our forefathers because we owe the greatness of Rome to it. If truth cannot be known by wise and learned men, it certainly cannot be known by ignorant Christians."

Octavius, the Christian, points out in his reply that all nature seems to speak of God and of God's existence. He says, "When you look at the heavens and everything around you, what is more obvious than that there must be an all-powerful God who sustains and controls all of nature? When you enter a house and see everything neatly arranged, you know that there is an owner who is greater by far than the things in the house. So isn't it obvious that there is a Lord far greater than the forces of nature?" Octavius then says that there can be only one God. If there were many gods, he reasons, they would continually fight among themselves and destroy the order in nature. Octavius ends by trying to show Caecilius that this one God must be the God in whom Christians believe. Caecilius admits that he is convinced by his friend's reasoning, and the two friends embrace.

In the conversation, the writer based Octavius's arguments on reason and the senses because Caecilius did not accept the Bible as absolutely true. It is said that Octavius was a real person, a friend of the writer Minucius Felix, and that the man died soon after having this conversation with a pagan friend.

4. Another famous Christian
   writer was Tertullian
   of Carthage. Tertullian
   served the Church
   by writing books
   which explained Christian
   beliefs and attacked
   false doctrines.
   But he was very strict,
   and he believed that people
   who sinned after Baptism
   should not be forgiven.

One of the great defenders of the Christian faith around the year 200 was another African named Tertullian. He was born in Carthage of pagan parents around 160. As a young man he devoted himself to study and the pursuit of pleasure. But he decided he wanted to discover a more worthwhile life. He went to Rome to practice law. There he saw the heroism of the Christian martyrs, and—inspired by them—he became a Christian around the year 195. He returned to Carthage around the year 200 and may have been ordained a priest.

A learned man, Tertullian was well equipped to challenge the views of the gnostics, people who believed that they alone possessed a special, secret knowledge (*gnosis*). Tertullian was fairly gentle toward heretics who led a good life, but he was harsh with those who used erroneous notions to justify their own immoral ways of living. (A *heretic* is a Christian who disagrees with accepted Church beliefs.) As a Christian apologist—a defender of the Christian point of view—Tertullian wrote many books. He pointed out the mistakes in pagan views and in the doctrines of heretical Christians. He also discussed how true Christians should think and act. Tertullian was quick-tempered and strict in his views. He felt that the Church should not pardon Christians who sinned. He believed that such people should be thrown out of the Church.

In the early part of the third century the heresy of Montanism was spreading. This school of thought rejected certain beliefs of the Church. Montanism favored a very strict way of life and rejected the God of the Old Testament. This point of view attracted Tertullian. After some years of doubt, he left the Christian Church and converted to Montanism in 213. But that did not fully satisfy him either, and he eventually formed his own group of followers, known as Tertullianists.

During Tertullian's time in Carthage, Christians and catechumens preparing for Baptism were arrested. The Roman emperor, Septimius Severus (193–211), had first been tolerant of Christianity and other eastern religions. But he grew worried when he realized that the new Christian religion was not just the faith of isolated individuals. He saw that it was bringing people together in a Church that became stronger every day. The growing organization of the Christian Church frightened him because it seemed to be a threat to the Roman empire.

The emperor hoped to break up the Church's organization by having Christians arrested and tried. Since Carthage had a strong Christian community, many arrests and trials took place there. Christians were ordered to sacrifice to the pagan gods and renounce their own God.

5. Christians in Carthage were persecuted in 193–211. Tertullian has left us the beautiful story of the martyrdom of Perpetua, a young mother.

Among those arrested in Carthage was a young noblewoman named Perpetua. A beautiful account of this young mother's martyrdom was written in Tertullian's time, perhaps by Tertullian himself. Most of the members of Perpetua's family were Christians, but her father was a pagan. Perpetua herself was arrested before she had actually received Baptism. Despite their religious differences, father and daughter loved each other very much. Perpetua's father visited her often in prison, trying to convince her to return to his traditional pagan religion.

On the day of Perpetua's trial, her father pleaded with her once more: "My daughter,

have pity on your white-haired father. Think of your brothers, your mother, your aunt, and your son who cannot live without you. Change your mind and don't ruin our whole family." The old man wept and pleaded with her. Perpetua grieved for her father's suffering, but she knew she could not renounce God for love of people. She tried to console her father with these words: "Understand that what will take place here is what is willed by God, the only master of our lives." Her words failed to console him.

A few days later, Perpetua's father came to see her again. He carried her baby boy in his arms. The Roman judge said, "Have pity on your old father and your little baby. Perform the sacrifice to our god!" Perpetua refused, declaring herself to be a Christian. Her weeping father clung to her until the procurator drove him off with a blow. "That blow," said Perpetua later, "hurt me as if I myself had been struck."

Perpetua was then taken to where she was to be killed. She knew that she was now close to Jesus, the only source of true joy. Her real sorrow was that her grieving father could not understand this because he did not share her Christian faith.

6. Titus Flavius Clement,
a Greek pagan in search
of religious truth,
became a Christian
around the year 190.
He became a well-known
teacher and writer
in the Christian school
of Alexandria.

Around the middle of the second century, Titus Flavius Clement was born of pagan parents in Athens. From his early youth he was eager to know the truth about life, and he studied religious questions carefully. Disappointed by the religious life of his native Greece, Clement moved to southern Italy in order to study under the famous philosophers there. But even they could not satisfy his thirst for truth. He set off for Syria, where many different oriental religions were popular. But the beliefs, secret mysteries, and magical practices of these religions did not satisfy him either. Clement moved on, this time to Palestine, but he did not find the answers to his questions there. So he continued his search.

At last Clement arrived in Alexandria, Egypt—one of the greatest cities in the Roman empire. Alexandria had a thriving port and was a bustling center of activity. There Clement found a Christian school for children and adults. Its leading teacher, Pantaenus, was a deeply religious person who became Clement's close friend. Clement's joy was great because Pantaenus seemed to be revealing the true meaning of life to him. After ten years, Clement became a Christian and

Pantaenus's chief assistant. He then began to work out a Christian theology.

Clement had learned many valuable things from his earlier pagan teachers, and he wanted to use this knowledge in the service of Christian truth. Having found what he was looking for, he wanted to share his faith with others. In his writings, Clement praised the elements of truth to be found in pagan thinking. But he tried to present the Christian faith with enthusiasm and with sincere respect for others' views so that non-Christian readers would want to discuss the subject with him.

Pantaenus died around 200, and Clement became the director of the Alexandrian school. He and later members of the school tried to reconcile Greek ideas and Christian teaching—that is, clear up the differences between Greek and Christian thinking. In this work they may have been influenced by the example of Philo, who had tried to reconcile Greek ideas and Jewish teaching in the first century. Persecution forced Clement to leave Alexandria around 202 or 203, and he never returned. He lived the rest of his life in the Christian community of Caesarea in Cappadocia (Asia Minor) and served the Church there. He died around 215.

7. Origen of Alexandria
was also a great teacher.
He planned and wrote
his own courses
on Christianity.
Origen became one
of the greatest
Christian thinkers and
teachers of his time.

Another great teacher in Alexandria was Origen, who devoted his whole adult life to teaching and exploring the Christian faith. Born in Alexandria around 185, Origen received his first lessons in the Christian faith from his parents. His father, Leonidas, also taught him how to profess the faith bravely. Leonidas died a martyr, and Origen never forgot his father's example. Origen decided to dedicate his life to the service of the Church.

After his father's death, the family property was taken by the government. Origen began to teach grammar in order to support his family. His pupils soon began to admire

his learning and his teaching ability. He did not teach grammar for long. Some of his pagan and Christian friends expressed an interest in learning more about Christianity, and so Origen decided to offer his own courses on the subject. He continued to study pagan and Christian thought himself, and to visit Christian communities in other countries. After some time, Origen was ordained a priest in Jerusalem.

When Origen was eighteen, Bishop Demetrius asked him to teach in the Christian school in Alexandria. For twenty-eight years, the school continued to make progress under Origen's guidance. But then Origen was accused of teaching errors and was banished from Alexandria. He moved to Caesarea, Palestine, and started a new school there. During the persecution by the emperor Decius, Origen bravely endured torture and died around 254.

Origen was probably the greatest Christian thinker of his time. He had great influence over his students because of his fine mind, extensive learning, and teaching ability. Origen's writings—particularly about the Bible—filled many books. Only a few of these books have come down to us today.

8. The teachings of Origen attracted pagans who were looking for a reason for life and a hope of something better after death. In this chapter, we begin an imaginary story about Aristos, a young man of Alexandria who heard Origen speak.

Aristos woke up feeling dejected. "What's wrong with me?" he wondered. "I have lots of friends and a good home. Why do I feel so dejected?"

Aristos thought about the party he had gone to the night before. It had become rather wild and he had left before it was over. Now he thought, "What's the use of living like that? Something is missing from my life."

Aristos left his house and ambled down to the Mediterranean Sea. There he spotted a ship on the vast waters. "It's going somewhere," Aristos thought. "It isn't just drifting along as I am."

A feeling of aimlessness swept through Aristos. His life seemed to have no meaning and no joy. He knew he was floating through life like a ship with no rudder.

Then Aristos thought about the new religion. There was a rumor that Christianity explained why people were given this life on earth and where they went after death. Christians even talked about a man who had risen from the dead! "Could that be?" Aristos asked himself. "Could that *really* be possible?"

There was talk in the city about a new teacher, Origen, who taught at the Christian school. Aristos glanced back at the ship that was headed out to sea. He turned away from the beach with his mind made up. He would go and hear this teacher, this man Origen he had heard about.

Aristos went to the school. The crowd listened quietly as Origen spoke. "You are not forced to live as a slave to sin and fate," he insisted. There was fierce conviction in the teacher's words. "How can you create a better life? How can you find peace? You do it by winning your freedom from sin!"

As Aristos left, he felt puzzled by these new ideas—yet he was excited, too. Someone yelled, "Wait for me!" and a stranger about his own age ran toward him.

"I'm Adeodatus," said the stranger. "I saw you at Origen's lecture. You looked confused. I've been baptized a Christian, so maybe I can help."

"Why should he care about me?" Aristos wondered. He stared for a long time at the friendly stranger. At last he said, "Maybe you can help me."

"Come to my house, then," said Adeodatus. "I want you to meet my father, and we will talk."

9. Aristos, the young man
in our story, became
a catechumen, which is
a person who is studying
to become a Christian.
As a catechumen,
he took part
in the prayer service
of the liturgy
and did charitable works.
On Easter Sunday,
he was baptized.

Years passed after Aristos's first meeting with a Christian. A deep friendship grew between Aristos and the Christian named Adeodatus. At last the time came when Aristos decided to become a Christian. But first he would have to be a catechumen and learn about the Christian faith. Aristos met and talked with Bishop Demetrius of Alexandria. "Aristos, you must have a Christian sponsor," explained the bishop. "And you must also tell the teacher of the catechumens why you want to become a Christian."

After his talk with the bishop, Aristos visited Adeodatus and his family. He asked Adeodatus's father to be his sponsor. Monica, Adeodatus's sister, made sesame candy to celebrate the happy decision.

Aristos now began the long period of instruction in the Christian faith. He visited the sick and saw the importance of works of charity. As Aristos studied the Bible, he learned more about faith. He attended the first part of the liturgy, where he prayed with the Christian community and listened to the word of God in Scripture readings and the homily. But Aristos could not stay for the eucharistic service because he had not yet been baptized.

Sometimes it seemed to Aristos that Easter and the time for Baptism would never come. But the day came closer. He met again with the bishop, who asked questions and encour-

aged Aristos in his studies.

On the evening before Easter, Aristos prayed through the night with other Christians. Then at dawn, all the catechumens approached the baptismal font. One of the first things they had to do was to say no to Satan and all things evil. Aristos felt the strength of his friends and teachers. Their prayers were with him as he renounced Satan.

As the ceremony continued, the bishop poured water over Aristos's head. "Do you believe in God, the Father almighty?" asked the bishop.

"I do," replied Aristos as the cleansing waters splashed over him.

"Do you believe in Jesus Christ, the son of God, born of the Virgin Mary through the Holy Spirit?"

"I do," replied Aristos.

"Do you believe in the Holy Spirit, the holy catholic Church and the resurrection of the dead?"

"I do," replied Aristos—and he no longer felt adrift.

The baptismal water, the words, and the bishop's kiss of peace completed the Baptism. Then, as a full-fledged Christian, Aristos went with the other newly baptized to take part in the Eucharist for the first time.

10. As a baptized Christian, Aristos now celebrated the Eucharist with other Christians.

Now that he had become a Christian, Aristos often took part in the liturgy. One Sunday morning it was still dark as he hurried along the deserted city streets to the home of a Christian. When he entered, the room was already crowded with Christians gathering to celebrate the liturgy. Adeodatus and Monica were there, and Aristos felt happy to see them.

Friendly talk soon gave way to music. The joyous sounds of the hymns and canticles seemed to wrap Aristos in warmth and friendship.

After the singing, Aristos listened intently to the deacon who read from the Bible, to the priest who gave the final reading, and to the bishop who preached the homily. Then came the prayers—prayers for those present, for the newly baptized, for the Church around the world, for the sick. Soon it was time for the kiss of peace. Aristos turned and fondly embraced his brothers and sisters in the faith.

Next came the eucharistic part of the liturgy, a service of giving thanks to God. The bishop and the priests extended their hands over the bread and wine presented by the dea-

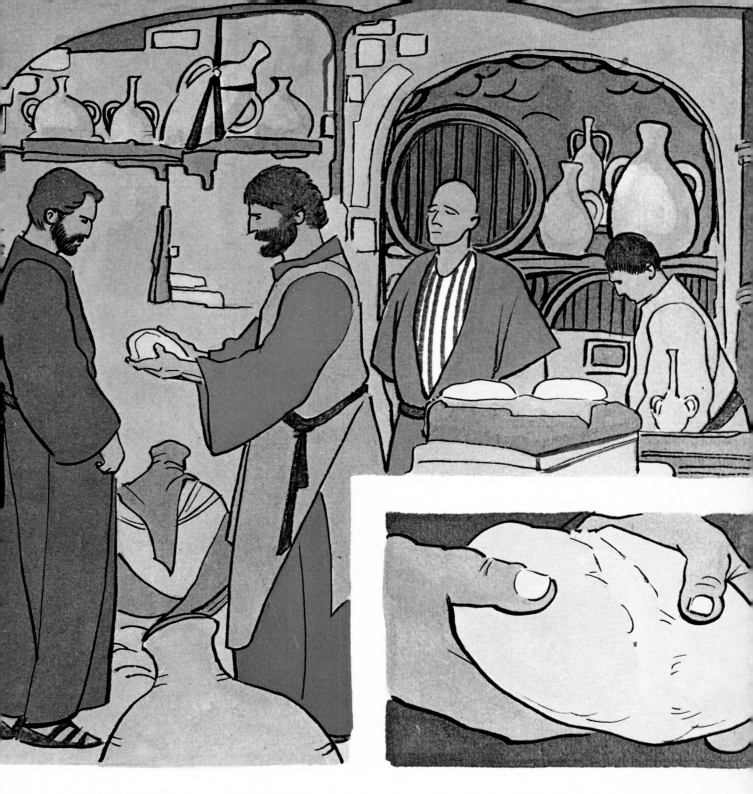

cons. During the prayer of thanksgiving to God for sending his Son Jesus, Aristos silently whispered, "Thank you, God, for the gift of faith."

After the bishop asked God to send the Holy Spirit on the faithful and their offerings, he consecrated the bread and wine. Following the consecration, Aristos joined in raising his hands to heaven and reciting, "Our Father, who art in heaven, hallowed be thy name. . . . "

Now it was time to approach the Eucharist, to receive the Bread and Wine that had become the Body and Blood of Jesus. His heart filled with peace, Aristos joined the other Christians at the table where the priests distributed the consecrated Bread and Wine. Later, the deacons would take the Eucharist to those sick at home.

The bishop gave a final blessing and the liturgy was over. But Aristos did not want to go home quite yet. He stayed to talk with his Christian friends. Adeodatus watched Monica and Aristos talk together happily. He was sure that they loved each other and would marry one day.

11. Our story describes
Aristos's work
in his father's shop,
where he helped make
papyrus sheets.
Papyrus was the material
on which people wrote
in those long-ago days,
as we today write on paper.

Aristos worked in his father's papyrus shop. One day he was surprised to see his friend Adeodatus walk in. "I thought I'd come to see what keeps you so busy on work days," he told Aristos.

Aristos showed his friend a piece of writing material called papyrus. "My father and I make these sheets from the papyrus reeds that grow along the Nile," said Aristos. Then he led Adeodatus to the workroom where the reeds were cut into strips and soaked in water. "Water softens the fibers of the papyrus plant," Aristos explained. "Then we put strips together to form sheets."

"But how do you get those long rolls?" Adeodatus questioned as he looked at a basket full of scrolls.

"We cut the papyrus into squares and paste them together. We can make a roll long enough for someone to write a whole book." Aristos knew that Adeodatus had seen the books of the Bible written on papyrus. "If you write only on one side, it's easy to unroll and read."

Aristos told his friend to look closely at how the sheet was formed and to feel it with his fingers. On one side, the fibers ran from side to side, making it easier for the writer to use a

pen than on the other side, where the fibers ran up and down.

Adeodatus looked around the busy workshop. "Don't you make parchment here, too?"

Aristos shook his head. "That costs more. And to make parchment you must take the skin of a sheep. Killing animals is not for me. Besides, most of our customers like papyrus better."

"You seem happy. Do you like working here?" asked Adeodatus.

"Yes, I do," Aristos answered, smiling as he spoke. "And I see work as a way of praising our God." It made Aristos feel good to think

of people far away listening to God's word read from a scroll made from papyrus right here in this shop.

"How long will you work with your father?"

"I don't know," Aristos said. "Sometimes I think of doing other work. But I have learned much here from my father and also from the merchants I meet. Meeting people gives me a chance to spread Christ's message."

12. Aristos and Monica,
two young people
in our story
of early Christian times
in Alexandria,
married each other.
The bishop blessed
their marriage.
Aristos's parents
decide to become
Christian.

Monica and Aristos became engaged soon after Aristos' Baptism. Now it was their wedding day. "Have I forgotten anything?" Aristos worried. In the excitement he must surely have overlooked something.

Aristos felt that everyone could hear the loud beat of his heart as he waited for the ceremony to begin. At last the time came. At the beginning of the eucharistic liturgy, Aristos and Monica took each other as man and wife in the sacrament of Marriage.

Looking at the young couple, the bishop blessed their action. "Remember," he said, "your union is to be a building stone of the Church. Your marriage today reminds us of the union of Christ and his Church. Respect and love each other faithfully. Be quick to forgive. And remember always that your bodies are temples of the Holy Spirit."

Then the bishop spoke about loving and respecting any children Aristos and Monica might have. Aristos prayed that he would one day be a father. "If I am, I will share my faith with my child as others have shared with me," he promised himself.

After the bishop finished speaking, Aristos and Monica took part in the Eucharist as husband and wife. The liturgy ended with a hymn of thanksgiving.

Friends and relatives then went to the small house where Monica and Aristos were to make their home. Happy sounds filled the air. There was the singing, dancing, and talking of the adults and the laughter of children playing games. As his parents congratulated him, Aristos said, "Mother, you seem especially happy today."

Aristos's parents looked at each other. Then his father said, "We have seen how happy you and Monica are as Christians. So we have spoken with the bishop. We, too, plan to be baptized."

Aristos was so filled with joy he did not know how he could be happier. But a few months later he learned that his prayer to become a father would be answered. Soon after their first anniversary, he and Monica had a baby boy.

13. In the early days of the Church, Christians did public penance for their sins. This is shown in the story of Aristos's repentance after a fight with a merchant.

Monica and Aristos's son had been ill, but at last there was no more crying. The house was quiet. "Maybe our son is getting over his sickness," Aristos whispered.

"He is still weak," Monica replied softly, "but sleep will strengthen him."

Aristos felt worn out himself. He had not slept well for a week, and it was hard to drag himself to work.

When Aristos got to the shop, a merchant was waiting. "How many papyrus plants do you want from me?" the merchant asked.

"None from you!" snapped Aristos. "You cheated me on the last order!"

"I sent what you paid for!" the merchant yelled back.

Aristos shoved the merchant. "Cheat!" he cried. Suddenly he punched the man. He hit him again and again. Other workers rushed to stop Aristos, but not soon enough. He had already injured the merchant.

Suddenly Aristos calmed down. "What have I done?" he asked himself. Feeling ashamed, he helped the merchant up and took him to his home. There he fed him and let him rest. "I'm sorry," Aristos apologized. "I've been worried about my son. When I saw you today, I just blew up."

"It's all right," said the merchant.

As soon as he could, Aristos went to his bishop. He told him the terrible thing he had done. "It is good that you are sorry," said the bishop. "Now you must pray and fast and do works of charity to atone. Then come back and I will give you the Lord's blessing."

Aristos went to the merchant and begged for his forgiveness. The merchant had in fact cheated Aristos, and now he was deeply moved. "We must end this fight," said the merchant. "From now on I will treat you fairly."

After that Aristos spent each evening in prayer, asking God's forgiveness. When he felt ready, he went to the place where the Eucharist was to be celebrated. He knelt outside, asking all who came to the service to pray for him.

When the liturgy ended, the bishop summoned Aristos. He placed his hands on Aristos's head as a sign of pardon and blessed him. "Be a man of peace, Aristos," the bishop said. "Now go and sin no more."

14. Fasting and good works were part of Christianity from the earliest times. In this part of the story of Aristos, he and his friend discuss fasting as penance for sin and praise for God.

One morning Aristos and Adeodatus went with a group of workers to help harvest papyrus reeds growing along the Nile river. At lunchtime, the workers stopped to rest and eat. But Aristos and Adeodatus weren't eating today. It was Friday and they were fasting. It was their way of doing penance and praising God.

The two friends hurried to the home of a Christian friend who was ill. "It is good of you to come and visit me," said the man as he set aside a container of soup. "Please excuse me for eating today."

"You have been ill and must eat to care for your body," Aristos said. "As the Bible says, there is a time for everything—a time for fasting and for eating."

"Everyone is praying that you will be well again soon," Adeodatus said.

"That is kind of them," the sick man said. Then, looking up at his visitors, he asked,

"What do the other workers say when you do not eat with them?"

"They don't notice what we do," said Adeodatus.

"Our fasting is a personal matter," explained Aristos. "It teaches us to be humble. I have learned that I can give up things I thought I couldn't do without." Aristos remembered fasting to do penance for his sins. And he recalled his days as a catechumen. Then he and the other catechumens had fasted before receiving Baptism.

Aristos bent down beside the sick man. "I pray that you will be well before Easter. Then we may fast together on those days which recall Jesus' passion."

"But on Easter we shall end our fast and celebrate his resurrection!" said Adeodatus. With that, he and Aristos ended their visit and went back to the reed cutters.

15. Easter was the most important Christian feast in the third century, just as it is today. Our story of Aristos ends with a description of his Easter celebration.

"What Origen told us is true," Aristos thought, "and now at Easter we celebrate the glorious resurrection of Jesus from the dead."

The light of dawn colored the eastern sky. It was time for the catechumens to be baptized. Aristos still remembered his own Baptism. With great hope, he joined them now to renew his vow, saying no to all things evil and yes to Jesus. Aristos knew that in many other parts of the world, Christians were gathering this morning to celebrate the

Easter was the happiest night of the year for Aristos, Monica, Adeodatus, and their Christian friends. They moved quickly through the streets of Alexandria to the home where they were to gather for the vigil of Easter, the most important Christian feast.

Songs and hymns filled the evening. Aristos found it hard to believe that he had once felt adrift. Today, as he listened to Old and New Testament readings, he felt direction and purpose in his life. The lines from the Psalms the Christians recited were the prayers of the ancient Israelites. "Now they are the prayers of the Christian Church itself," Aristos thought.

As the people awaited Easter, Aristos realized that God was with each person there.

Eucharist just as he and his friends were here in Alexandria. He liked the feeling of being part of a large community spreading around the world.

When the service ended, Aristos and the others went out to feast together. Easter was a time to rejoice with Christian friends, sharing food and talk and praising God in song and dance.

Today, as in Alexandria in the second century, Christians use Old Testament Psalms as prayers. Many Christians use verses from Psalm 118 to rejoice at Easter and to praise God's goodness.

I shall not die, but I shall live,
    and recount the deeds of the Lord. . . .
This is the day which the Lord has made;
    Let us rejoice and be glad in it. . . .
O give thanks to the Lord for he is good;
    for his steadfast love endures forever.
Psalm 118: 17, 24, 29

EPIPHANY

CHRISTMAS

16. At this time, the Church begin to organize the yearly calendar around great holy days. By 350, the periods of time for celebrating Christmas, Easter, and Pentecost were established.

After the year 200, the Church developed more fully its calendar of feasts, which set aside special days to recall important events in the lives of Jesus and his apostles. This led to more careful organization of the liturgy, the Church's formal worship of God, because some prayers in the liturgy centered on the feast days.

The passion, death, and resurrection of Jesus were celebrated from the very beginning, and so was Pentecost. As the liturgy became better organized, the celebrations of the Easter period were given more formal shape. For fifty days after Easter Sunday the Church celebrated its joy at the resurrection of Christ. Christians stopped fasting and prayed standing up rather than kneeling down. The liturgy

PENTECOST

EASTER

gave special attention to newly baptized Christians during the week after Easter. On the fiftieth day after Easter, the Church celebrated Pentecost, marking the close of the Easter period and recalling the descent of the Holy Spirit upon the apostles. Ten days before Pentecost, the Church recalled the Ascension of Jesus to his Father. This feast was placed shortly before Pentecost to remind people that Jesus did not leave his followers alone—that he sent the Holy Spirit to guide the Church.

From the middle of December to January 6, Christians celebrated another important period, recalling Jesus' birth. Around 230, Christians in Rome began to celebrate the birth of Jesus (Christmas) on December 25. This feast

was slow to become popular. Armenia refused to accept that date and continued to celebrate Christ's birth on January 6. In other regions, January 6 became the feast of the Epiphany, celebrating the public manifestation or showing forth of Jesus to the Magi.

The Church also remembered the apostles, martyrs, and saints who had followed the example of Jesus with great love and generosity. Local Christian communities remembered their own martyrs by celebrating the liturgy at a martyr's grave on the anniversary of his or her death, which also marked the date of the martyr's birthday in heaven. Christians felt they should imitate the saints. They regarded the saints as friends in heaven who would ask God to help Christians on earth.

17. Though Christians
sometimes argued
among themselves,
they tried to live up
to the promises
they had made at Baptism.
Pagans were impressed
by the way Christians
helped people in need.
Many Christians
gave up family life
in order to serve
the Church.
Some even suffered
martyrdom for the faith.

By the third century, Christians were no longer a small group. The world saw the Church growing and spreading. The new Christian way of life attracted the attention of many people. Some thought the growing Christian Church was becoming a danger to the Roman Empire.

Christians themselves knew that they had been baptized into a new way of life, even though they did not always live up to its ideals. They often reflected on the meaning of their Baptism. Origen, for example, told Christians that their new life begun at Baptism was directed by Jesus and that they should follow no one but him. Christians should remain faithful to their new way of life and keep growing in it, he said. Origen compared Christians to grapes on a vine: they should keep growing until they were completely ripe and juicy.

While Christians could be selfish and at times took part in harsh arguments, they nevertheless tried hard to overcome their sinfulness and to express their faith by their actions. They were willing to suffer martyrdom gladly, if that should be necessary—and it often was during the third century. Though some Christians denied their faith, many re- mained loyal even if that meant death. These Christians felt that Jesus himself was suffering with them. This made death seem less fearful to them.

Many Christians were willing to give generously of themselves even when there was no threat of martyrdom. When disease and plague attacked people, Christians often cared for the sick and the dying, whoever they might be. Some Christians chose not to have families of their own but to dedicate themselves to the service of the Church. Another expression of Christian faith which was highly regarded was charity toward the needy. Many Christians tried to help the very old and the very young, orphans and widows, travelers and needy strangers. They also buried the dead—even those who were strangers to them. These acts of charity were looked on as signs of one's faithfulness to Baptism.

In the Church, slaves were on equal footing with other Christians. While the Church did not yet actively work to end slavery, its care and concern for slaves was an important step forward. This loving care which Christians showed one another amazed many pagans, who could not help exclaiming, "See how they love one another!"

18. The Roman Empire had many problems around the year 200. Barbarian tribes warred against Rome. Roman army commanders fought each other, and often army leaders were elected emperor. High taxes and poor trade made people worry, and many people became hopeful at the idea of a savior-god.

For two centuries the Roman empire had enjoyed wealth, luxury, and power. Many people regarded it as the only true civilization. But a number of problems became increasingly serious during the third century.

Until this time, the empire had not had to worry greatly about the various peoples living outside its borders. But now tribes and nations began to threaten the boundaries of the empire. The Persians posed a threat in Asia Minor, the Berbers in North Africa, the Picts in Scotland, and several German tribes along the Rhine River and the Danube River in Europe.

Many soldiers in the Roman army were barbarians who had become Roman citizens or allies. Commanders of troops fought each other to gain power, and after bloody wars such military leaders quite often became emperor. One emperor quickly replaced another.

This unrest helped to make other problems worse. Heavy taxes were imposed on the population. Trade decreased, and there was constant worry about supplying food to people in the cities. Sickness and plague may also have grown more serious during this period.

The overall situation caused much unhappiness, and people began to think more about

their personal problems and the meaning of life.

A few noble Romans and others accepted the ideals of Stoicism—a philosophy that taught people to live in agreement with the law of nature and to master their own thoughts. Most people, however, grew more interested in religious ideas, particularly those that offered the possibility of personal salvation and eternal life.

Eastern religions and secret rites with an air of mystery attracted some Romans. For example, the worship of Mithra, originally a god of Persia and India, became very popular in the Roman army. Mithra, it was said, fearlessly fought the powers of evil and promised eternal life to his followers.

Although the secret ritual of Mithraism was restricted to men, other cults were open to women as well. People traveled far to participate in rites that promised eternal life and salvation. Troubled times probably helped to increase interest in the idea of a savior-god, an idea which had developed since around 200 B.C. in many religions.

19. In 250, the emperor ordered all citizens to worship the gods by offering sacrifice. Those who refused were condemned to death. Many Christians were killed in this persecution.

In 250, the emperor Decius issued an edict ordering all citizens of the empire to take part in a general sacrifice to the gods of Rome. Various committees were organized to make sure the edict was carried out. Each person who performed the sacrifice was given a certificate called a *libellus*. After a certain length of time, the certificates were presented to the authorities. Those who had refused to perform the sacrifice were thrown into prison. Torture and other means were used to make

them change their minds. Those who still refused to sacrifice were killed. Many Christians decided to shed their blood rather than give up Christ. Other Christians, however, chose to save themselves by giving up Christ and performing the sacrifice.

The edict brought suffering and death to many Christians, as the persecution was carefully organized. Decius may have wanted to destroy the Christian Church completely in order to strengthen the empire. The persecu-

tion did not last long, but it was very severe.

In the end, the emperor failed to destroy the Church. Though the persecution was unexpected, Christians soon began to prepare spiritually for martyrdom. Men, women, and children who went to prison began to look forward to their final reunion with Jesus. The threat of suffering and death could not make them change their minds. As a pagan writer of the time put it: "The blood of martyrs is a seed from which new Christians spring."

20. Many Christians caught in the persecution by Decius gave up their Christian faith for fear of suffering and death.

Later, some of them were sorry and asked to be forgiven. After doing penance, they were received back into the Christian community.

As we noted, not all Christians had the courage to undergo martyrdom. Some bribed members of the committees and received certificates (*libelli*) even though they had not performed the sacrifice. These people were known as *libellatici*. Some burned incense before the statues of the gods or the emperor, and because a person who carries incense is called a *thurifer*, these people were known as *thurificati*. All those who had betrayed the faith in one way or another were called *lapsi*, because they had slipped or lapsed from the faith.

When the persecution ended, large numbers of the lapsi asked to be taken back into the Christian community. This was a difficult problem for the Church to resolve. On the one hand, the sin of betraying the faith was very serious. On the other hand, Jesus had set an example by forgiving Peter after Peter had denied him three times. Some Christians insisted that lapsi should not be taken back into the Church. When Church authorities decided to pardon lapsi, these Christians refused to accept the decision and finally ended up outside the Church.

In seeking pardon, some lapsi presented letters on their behalf which had been written by Christian martyrs before they died. The church authorities were lenient on the certificate-holders, the libellatici, who had not really betrayed the Christian faith. After being examined, the libellatici were granted "peace," which meant they could come back into the Christian community.

It was harder for the thurificati because they had really fallen away from the faith. If they admitted their guilt publicly and showed that they were sorry for what they had done, they could be received back into the Church if they were in danger of death. Otherwise these people could enter the Church only after a period of penance. Church authorities decided what the penance would be. Usually these sinners had to wear the clothes of a penitent, pray, and do works of mercy.

After a period of penance the sinners asked their bishop, the local priests, and the community to take them back. The bishop granted pardon by laying his hands on the penitent's head. The Church was careful to rebuke sinners, but also showed love and mercy and pardoned wrongdoing.

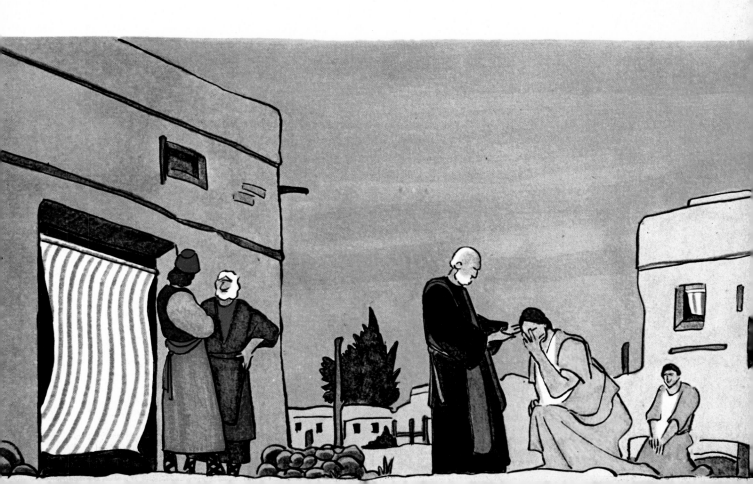

21. Pope Fabian was one of the first martyrs in the persecution by Decius. Fabian had been very active in organizing the Christian community in Rome, and Decius feared his power. Fabian was arrested and condemned to death when he refused to give up his faith.

One of the first victims of the persecution by Decius was Pope Fabian, who had been elected pope in January 236. Fabian did his work energetically and fearlessly. During the brief period of peace that followed the death of Emperor Maximin of Thrace in 238, Fabian reorganized the Christian community around Rome.

The city had previously been divided into fourteen districts. Fabian divided it into only seven districts and put a deacon in charge of each one. He also showed concern for Christian cemeteries in Rome. He had the remains of his dead predecessor, Pope Pontian, brought to Rome from Sardinia and placed beside the grave of another pope in the Callistus cemetery. For a long time afterward, popes would be buried in this cemetery.

Fabian also exchanged letters with Origen in Alexandria, but their letters have not been preserved.

The organizational work of Pope Fabian greatly angered Decius, and he declared Fabian an enemy of the empire. This was a death threat which the emperor quickly carried out. At the start of the persecution, Fabian was one of the first to be condemned. This successor of St. Peter gave up his life for the Church, even as Jesus had done. To Fabian, martyrdom was simply part of his total self-giving to Christ. He accepted death calmly on January 20, 250.

Christians living far away from Rome received letters announcing the pope's martyrdom. The community of the Church all over the known world gathered to pray.

22. The emperor Valerian
continued the persecution
begun by Decius.
In 258, Pope Sixtus
was martyred
as he said Mass
in a catacomb.
Lawrence, the last deacon
left alive in Rome,
was caught and killed.
Thus the emperor tried
to destroy the Church
by killing its leaders.
But the Church lived on.

Valerian became emperor in 253, and in 257 he began to persecute Christians. He did not allow Christians to meet for religious worship or to visit their cemeteries.

On August 6, 258, the persecution became more severe. Pope Sixtus II, assisted by some of his deacons, was secretly saying Mass in the beautifully decorated Roman catacomb of St. Callistus. He knew that the emperor forbade this under threat of death, but Sixtus's love for Christ was stronger than his fear of the emperor. Suddenly the voices and quick steps

of Roman soldiers could be heard in the passageways. They saw that the pope and his deacons were celebrating the Eucharist. Sixtus and his deacons were put to death on the spot.

The terrible persecution spread quickly through the Church of Rome. Of the seven deacons who took care of the various Church districts, soon only one, Lawrence, remained alive. He, too, was arrested. The Roman authorities demanded to know where the Church treasury under his care was to be found. They killed Lawrence when he refused to tell them. Lawrence was not concerned about keeping the money. He knew that the Roman emperor was trying to destroy the Church by killing its leading figures, taking over its goods and property, and thus creating despair among the faithful. He wanted to stand firm for the Church against its enemies.

The emperor was not successful in destroying the Church, but many people died before the persecution was over.

23. Cyprian of Carthage was another great defender of the faith who lived at this time. A rich and learned pagan, Cyprian startled people when he became a Christian. In 248 he became bishop of Carthage.

Just about the time Tertullian left the Church, another great upholder of the faith—Cyprian—was living in Carthage. Cyprian was born between 200 and 210 into a rich and cultured family. After his studies, he gained a great reputation in Carthage for his ability as a speaker and a teacher of oratory. But he led a thoughtless life, devoting himself to pleasure and idolatrous practices.

At some point, Cyprian grew sick of the immorality and corruption that he saw everywhere around him. A priest named Caecilius helped Cyprian search for truth. Cyprian became a Christian and gave his goods away to the poor. To the pagans, Cyprian's conversion

was a scandal. To Christians, it seemed nothing less than a miracle.

This man who had loved a life of ease and pleasure now urged people to respect and love each other and themselves. Cyprian gave up his wealth and the studies he had once loved in order to concentrate on the true wisdom that came from God. The Bible now became his favorite reading. He also loved the writings of Tertullian, and he often asked his servant for the works of "the master."

Having found the life he was seeking, Cyprian devoted himself to it completely and was ordained a priest. In his own writings of this period, Cyprian praised the spiritual rebirth brought by Christianity and condemned the corrupt living of pagans. He insisted that Christian law was superior to Jewish law, and he spoke of Christ as the true God and Redeemer of human beings.

In 248 Carthage needed a new bishop and there was talk of appointing Cyprian. Some older priests had doubts. Cyprian had not been a Christian for very long, and his earlier way of life had not been inspiring. But the Christian people of Carthage made their voices heard, and Cyprian was chosen. Years of harsh suffering lay ahead for the new bishop and the church of Carthage.

24. Bishop Cyprian sometimes disagreed with the pope, but he also seemed to believe that the pope's power went far beyond Rome. Cyprian felt that Church unity was very important, and he wrote a famous book about it.

Cyprian was one of the first Christian writers to assert that the Church in Rome had a place of special importance among Christian churches. In one of his written works, Cyprian described the diocese of Rome as the "chair of Peter and the principal Church, from which comes priestly unity."

In an important work called *The Unity of the Church*, Cyprian said that our Lord founded the first Church on one person, Peter, and that this was a pattern for all time. Cyprian also called on Christians to work for unity in their local churches and to be obedient and faithful to their bishop.

A year later, Cyprian heard of a serious problem. Marcion, bishop of Arles in what is today France, refused to grant pardon to lapsi, even if they were repentant and were dying. Lapsi were Christians who had given up their religion during times of persecution. The Church had ruled that they could be received back into the Church only after years

of penance, though repentant lapsi who were in danger of death could be pardoned at once. But Bishop Marcion refused to grant pardon.

Now Cyprian appealed to the pope as someone with authority over Bishop Marcion. He wrote to Pope Stephen and asked him to depose Marcion—that is, to remove him from his position as bishop. Thus, Cyprian showed that he believed that the power of the pope went beyond Rome.

In this case, Cyprian supported the authority of the pope, though at other times he argued with the pope. But throughout his life, Cyprian valued Church unity as a precious gift. He never said that he thought that the bishop of Rome had the authority to govern, in the modern sense, the whole Church. But he did recognize that the see or diocese of Rome had special importance because it was the see of the apostle Peter, who had been called by Christ to lead the apostles.

25. In the persecution of 257–58, the people of the Roman empire were again ordered to sacrifice to the gods. Christians were not allowed to go to their cemeteries or to celebrate the Eucharist. Cyprian was arrested and ordered to sacrifice. When he would not, he was beheaded.

When Decius began persecuting Christians in 250, Cyprian was bishop of Carthage. He loved his people. During a time of plague, Cyprian cared for the sick, risking his own health. In this period of persecution, Cyprian felt that his people needed him alive, so he left Carthage to escape being captured and killed. Christians did not run blindly after martyrdom at all costs. They weighed the situation prudently, especially when others were concerned. Bishop Cyprian returned to Carthage in 251.

In the years 257–258, however, another persecution arose to torment the Church of Jesus. Again all were commanded to sacrifice to the Roman gods. Christians were forbidden to celebrate the Eucharist or to go to cemeteries. Roman senators and knights who had become Christians were stripped of their offices and ranks.

Cyprian remained with his people. In 258, Cyprian was arrested and taken to the summer residence of Galerius Maximus, a Roman proconsul. A large crowd had gathered in the proconsul's residence for Cyprian's trial. Cyprian was asked if he headed the Christian Church of Carthage, and he answered yes. He refused to sacrifice to the gods and was condemned to be beheaded.

Cyprian waited calmly for his death. When the executioner came, Cyprian asked his deacons to give the man twenty-five gold pieces. Cyprian was beheaded on September 14, 258, and his corpse was placed on the ground. During the night Christians bore it away in solemn, respectful procession, praising God for a new saint in heaven.

26. Between the years
200 and 300, Christians
began to think and write
more fully and deeply
about the Church.
They especially liked
to think of the Church
as the bride of Christ
and as Mother of all.
These two images
were a sign of the love
between Christ
and his Church,
and of the Church's
motherly care
for all the faithful.

During the third century, Christian writers began to think more seriously about the Church. They tried to understand what the Church was and to express this understanding of the Christian community. They wanted to know and love the Church more fully and to explain it more clearly to pagans.

Some writers described the Church as the bride or spouse of Christ. This comparison expressed how much Jesus loved the Church and reminded Christians to love their Savior in return. Moreover, Jesus supported, helped, and protected the Church like a faithful marriage partner. Like the bond of marriage, the bond between Christ and the Christian lasts a lifetime. In fact, Jesus promised to be with the Christian community always.

These third-century Christian writers were not the first to compare the bonds between Christ and the Church to the bonds of marriage. Writers of books in the Old and New Testaments used this image. The Song of Songs describes the love between God and Israel as like the love between man and woman. The apostle Paul exhorts husbands, "Love your wives, as Christ loved the Church"

SPONSA CHRISTI   MATER ECCLESIA

(Ephesians 5:25). The Book of Revelation describes the Christian community as "beautiful as a bride prepared to meet her husband" (21:2).

Images of married love and faithfulness helped Christians understand and express the love between Christ and the Church. This image expresses the bonds between each Christian and Christ, too. Each person is beloved of Jesus. Jesus gave up his life for all and loves each person.

Christians also began to describe the Church as the mother of all the faithful. Just as a father and mother gave life to their children, so Jesus and the Church gave new life to the baptized and enabled them to live as friends of God. Like a true mother, the Church gave spiritual nourishment to her children. She prayed for them and explained the words of Jesus to them so that they might journey safely and securely through life. And like a loving, kind mother, the Church was always ready to forgive her children their faults when they expressed sorrow for them.

27. Today in Rome
we can still visit
Christian cemeteries, or
catacombs. They are
underground galleries
or halls, with graves
of the dead placed
in the walls.
In times of persecution,
Christians gathered
in the catacombs
to celebrate the Eucharist.

The number of Christians was increasing greatly. Sometimes a local Church had too many members to gather in a private home, as had been the practice. So Christians began to set aside special places and buildings for the celebration of the Eucharist and prayer. They also set aside their own cemeteries for the burial of the dead. A historian in the fourth century used the word *catacombs* to describe these Christian cemeteries. *Catacomb* comes from a Greek word meaning "ravine." By the year 800, this term was widely used to describe underground Christian burial places.

The oldest catacomb in Rome is that of St. Callistus, named after the deacon who had been in charge of it. Many popes were buried there, but it was not the only Roman cemetery.

Every catacomb had different galleries, long halls which ran in several directions and at various depths under the ground. Along the walls of these galleries were *loculi,* holes carved out to hold the corpses of the dead. These graves were then covered over, and the dead person's name was placed on the outside. Sometimes the person's age was given, and Christian symbols were added. Besides the loculi, there were also larger areas where whole families might be buried together.

The inscriptions on these Christian graves expressed love for the dead and also praise of God and belief in the resurrection of the dead. Many of the paintings and other decorations in the catacombs also reminded Christians of salvation and the everlasting life of the soul.

The catacombs were meeting places as well as burial grounds. Christians met there to celebrate the Eucharist, particularly in times of persecution and on the feasts of martyrs buried there.

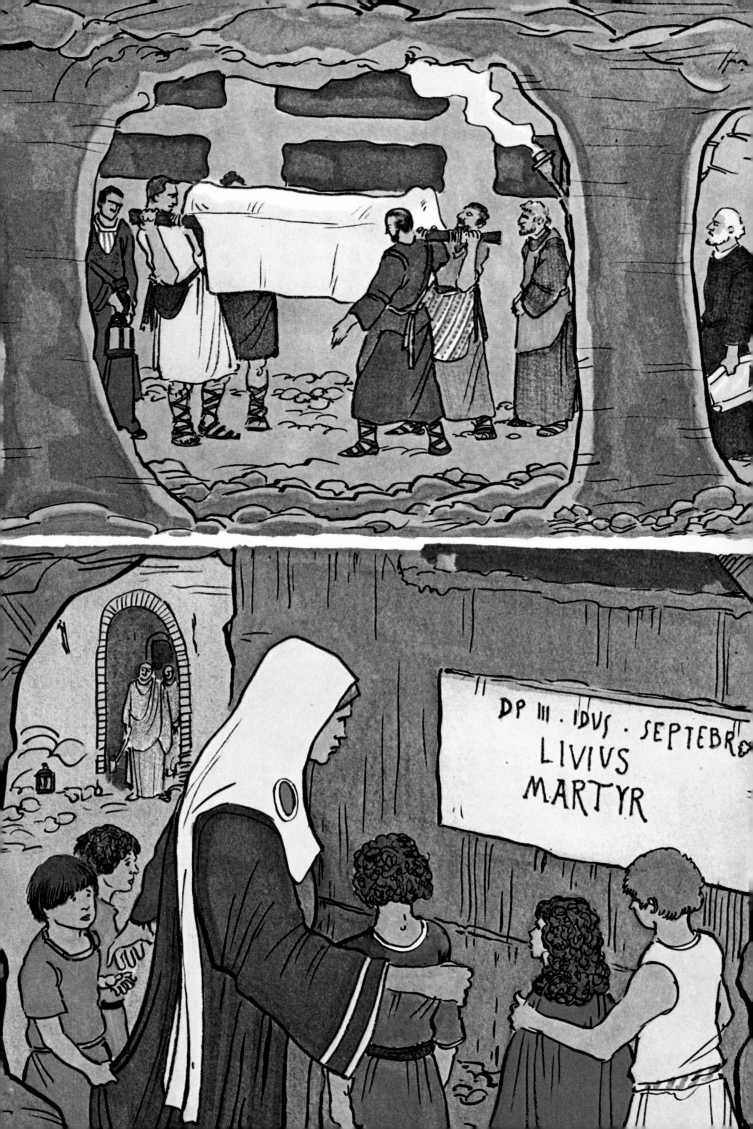

28. **Christian art developed and was used to decorate places of worship and burial grounds. Much Christian art could not be shown in public places because Christianity was a forbidden religion, persecuted by the emperor.**

At first Christians were doubtful about using religious images. Their Jewish background influenced them against making images of God, and they feared that people might worship images as deities. Art could be a temptation to idolatry, as some pagan worship showed. On the other hand, many Christians felt that creating beautiful art was a way of praising God. Art could also help express and symbolize the truths of faith and of the Bible. Gradually art was allowed in places of Christian worship as the Church tried to bring the basic ideas of faith in Jesus to life in her liturgy.

It is primarily in the catacombs that we find the first examples of Christian art. Christian images were not found in public places because Christianity was a forbidden religion. Christian art on the walls of the catacombs showed many favorite scenes from the Old Testament and the New Testament: Daniel in the lion's den; Noah and the Ark; Jonah and the whale; the raising of Lazarus from the dead by Jesus. Christians used scenes of liberation from death to express their faith in an eternal life free from evil and misery. Christian art often pictured Jesus. And since he led souls to heaven, he was often pictured as the Good Shepherd.

The early Christians often painted symbols instead of pictures. One of their favorite symbols was a fish, which they used as a kind of code word for the name "Jesus." The letters of the Greek word for fish (*ichthus*) were the first letters of the words in the Greek phrase "Jesus Christ, Son of God, Savior" (*iesus christos, theou uios, soter*).

Another favorite symbol used widely was a boat, which stood for the Church. On it Christians journeyed safely through the world, shown as the ocean, to their home port, the kingdom of heaven. The symbol of a fisherman was also used a great deal because Jesus told Peter and Andrew that he would make them fishers of people. The symbol expressed the Christian desire to preach Jesus' message to everyone.

Another symbol, the dove, had several meanings. The Bible records that at Christ's Baptism in the Jordan River, the Holy Spirit came to him in the form of a dove. Besides symbolizing the Spirit, the dove stood for the Church, for the individual soul striving toward God, and also for the purity that should mark both the Church and the individual Christian.

IMPERATOR CAESAR PUBLIUS LICINIUS. GALLIENUS PIUS FELIX AUGUSTUS DIONISYO ET PINNAE ET DEMETRIO ET CETERIS EPISCOPIS.

29. The Emperor Gallienus stopped the persecution of Christians in 260. For the next forty years, the Church had peace. It began to grow strong and to spread widely.

After many years of persecution which greatly tested Christian communities, a time of peace came. In 260 Gallienus became emperor. As an imperial officer, he had helped his father, the emperor Valerian, to persecute Christians. Perhaps he saw how wrong and cruel this had been, for he stopped the persecution of Christians when he became emperor. He issued an edict allowing Christians to live in peace. He gave back to Christians the property that had been taken away from them. He also gave back to the Church her places of worship. Many Christians returned to their government jobs, where they were often received back with great sympathy.

This imperial act was very important. It did not make Christianity a legally recognized religion, but it did show that the official Church had a right to exist. Moreover, for some forty years after this edict the Church was able to go about her work in peace. Christians could talk about their religion in public, advertise their religious services, conduct worship openly, build churches, and preach to people without fear of being killed.

Some pagans continued to speak out against Christianity or to write against it. But during this time, the new faith was able to spread widely.

30. During the time of peace after Gallienus stopped the persecution, Christians were eager to spread their faith. Missionary work was very successful in the East.

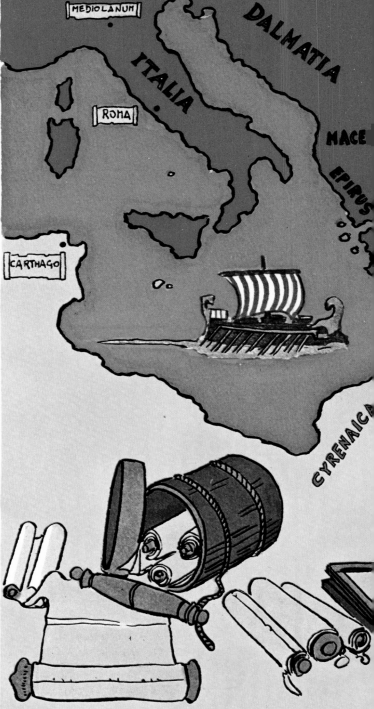

In the latter half of the third century, the Church began to spread farther and farther into distant lands. In the eastern part of the Roman empire, the center of this missionary movement was Alexandria, Egypt. Christianity soon spread throughout Egypt from there, reaching into small villages as well as large cities. At that time Greek and Coptic were the main languages spoken in Egypt. Because the first missionaries of Alexandria spoke Greek, they preached only to Greek-speaking people.

But soon Christianity also spread among those who spoke Coptic.

From Alexandria, missionaries headed out to convert northern Arabia, which is now Palestine. Jesus' homeland did not welcome missionaries enthusiastically. Although most of the Church's converts in Palestine were foreigners living there, in some cities the missionary work of Christians was quite successful.

The coastal areas of Syria now welcomed

the Gospel message. The great Christian community of Antioch was a center for missionary journeys. Edessa in Mesopotamia was also a Christian city during this period. From there missionary Christians set out to bring Christianity to the surrounding countryside. Going beyond the boundaries of the Roman empire, Christian missionaries also traveled to Persia and far-off India.

Various Christian communities in Asia Minor also sought to spread the message of Christ to the surrounding villages and rural areas. This was particularly true in Pontus, Cappadocia, Cilicia, and Armenia. The Gospel was also preached in the islands around Greece, in Cyprus especially. But mainland Greece was not as open to the Christian message. Along this route, however, the Gospel message reached the Crimea, an area on the northern shore of the Black Sea, now the southern tip of the Soviet Union.

31. Christianity spread more slowly in the West than in the East, but the number of Christians grew in the regions known today as Spain, Germany, and England.

Although Christianity spread more slowly in the West, the number of Christians began to grow. In Italy there was much missionary work. This was supported by the strong Christian community of Rome. Many Christian communities arose in northern Italy, in such places as Ravenna, Bologna, and Milan. Christianity also began to spread in Sicily and Sardinia.

In the region known today as France, Christianity began to flourish in the Rhone valley. The communities of Lyons and Arles were very strong, and the whole Provence region opened up to conversion. After 300 the western area between Bordeaux and Clermont-Ferrand was converted.

In the region now known as Germany, Christianity also began to have an influence, particularly around Mainz and Cologne. Missionaries were especially active along the lower Rhine River, and a large Christian community also arose in Augusta.

Even before 300 there were sizable groups of Christians in England. London, York, and Colchester were episcopal sees, or dioceses. But missionary work on a large scale took place only after 300.

In Spain, Christianity spread first in the southeast, then extended westward toward the Atlantic coast. There were Christian communities in such places as Cordova, Calahorra, and Sagunto. Many of them probably had their own bishops by this time. Between 200 and 300 Christianity spread to many parts of North Africa.

By 300, then, Christianity was spreading. Though only a small part of the people in the Roman empire were Christian, missionaries everywhere were laying the foundations for a bright future.

32. In 284, Diocletian became emperor. He did a great deal to reorganize and strengthen the empire. Under his rule, the emperor was revered as a god and had unlimited power.

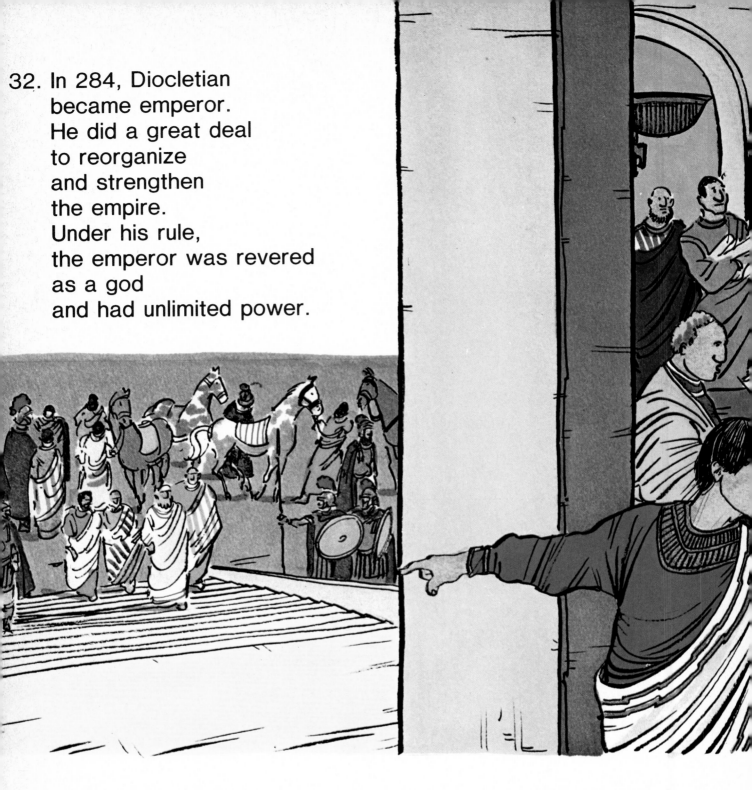

In 284, the officers of the Roman army in the East revolted. They proclaimed Diocletian, the commander of the imperial guard, emperor. This was not the first time that the army had decided who would be the emperor.

Diocletian wanted to reorganize the government and rebuild the strength of the Roman empire. He began by strengthening the power of the emperor.

Supposedly, the Roman senate ruled Rome, and the emperor acted as head of the government only during times of emergency. But in reality, the emperor ruled. Emperors succeeded one another, keeping their power to rule by pretending that the emergency was still going on.

Diocletian now made the emperor an absolute ruler with unlimited authority.

Eastern religions spreading in Rome helped support the idea of the emperor's power. These religions spoke of the emperor as divine, a god on earth. In homes, offices, and army headquarters, people burned candles around Diocletian's portrait, as though worshiping him. The emperor wore a crown of gold covered with pearls and a cloak embroidered with gold and precious jewels. Subjects knelt when he passed, and he was considered sacred.

Besides arousing awe and attention through religious beliefs, Diocletian became the center of the empire through his practical

measures. He reorganized the administration of the empire so that his laws would be followed from the largest city to the smallest village. He also reformed the army so that it could fight victoriously against the Persians in the East and the Germanic tribes in the West.

The number of civil and military officials grew enormously. They had special status in public life and enjoyed much power under the emperor. Police agents began to watch citizens closely.

All this required money, of course. Diocletian successfully reformed the tax and money system. He tried to keep careful records so that he would know exactly how much money was available. All sorts of taxes were laid on the people, and these taxes were collected without mercy.

Through all these means Diocletian managed to make the empire stronger. But the price was heavy for his subjects, who lost much of the personal freedom they had once enjoyed.

33. Diocletian thought that Christianity would undermine his reformed government. In 303 he began a terrible persecution that lasted eight years.

In 303, therefore, Diocletian issued a decree ordering the destruction of Christian churches and the burning of Christian sacred books. Many churches were destroyed and many members of the clergy were condemned to death.

A second edict deprived the Christian communities of their pastors. The prisons were so full of bishops, priests, and deacons that there was not enough room to hold them all. A third edict declared that the clergy who agreed to sacrifice to the Roman gods would be set free. Others would be tortured and put to death. A

In the early years of his reign, Diocletian continued the policy of tolerating Christians. At this time, many civil and court officials were Christians, and Diocletian seemed to have no fear of them. Diocletian himself was a follower of Mithra, as were many Roman soldiers.

All went well until around the year 300, when Diocletian had almost completed the work of reorganizing the government. Diocletian decided that it was now time to provide religion for his subjects. He wanted to uphold the old Roman type of religion, and he was given bad advice by Galerius, his chief helper. Galerius wanted to bring back the pagan religion and he made plans that would lead to death for many Christians. Galerius convinced Diocletian that Christianity might undermine the strength and solidity of his army and his government and endanger all his work.

fourth edict ordered all to sacrifice to the gods under penalty of death.

Mistreatment, torture, and killing began with the very first edict. Christians who had been working in the government were reduced to the status of slaves. Diocletian's own wife and daughter, who were suspected of being Christian, were forced to offer sacrifice. With the fourth edict the persecution took on gigantic proportions. A large number of Christians were put to death all over the empire.

The persecution ended unexpectedly.

Galerius, the person who had helped start the persecution, became emperor in 305. In 311, as he was dying, he joined with two other imperial rulers to issue a new edict saying that Christians could once again practice their religion. The rulers who wrote this decree were not in favor of Christianity. Instead, they were scornful of it. But they realized that the persecution was not bringing back the old religion. Instead, there were now many people who had no religion at all. This was bad for the government, and so the rulers decided to let Christianity exist again.

34. Many Christians
suffered and died
during the persecution
by Diocletian.
One of these saints
was a young girl, Agnes.
Her story is told here.

Not only adults but also children were put to death during the terrible persecution started by Diocletian. The most famous story of this period concerns Agnes, a girl of twelve. Agnes suffered martyrdom even though children her age were not held responsible before Roman law. She was probably a real person, but the story has come down to us in a rather legendary form.

When the persecution began, Agnes's parents feared for her safety and kept her at home. But she was not afraid and she did not want to betray Jesus. In vain her parents tried to tell her that one did not have to seek out

martyrdom, that one had an obligation to defend one's own life.

One day Agnes left the house, found some Roman soldiers; and professed her faith openly to them. She was taken into custody and questioned by the magistrate. He thought it would be easy to convince such a young girl to offer sacrifice. Neither his flattery nor his threats had any effect on Agnes. She seemed to have no fear of the punishments he described to her. Neither time in prison nor torture changed her mind, and legend tells us that an angel of the Lord protected her. The soldiers and judges felt compassion for the child, but the law forbade her release. She was led to her death on January 21, which today the Catholic Church celebrates as her feast day.

The name "Agnes" is much like the Latin word "agnus" meaning "lamb," and this probably explains why pictures of Agnes often show her with a lamb. On January 21, in the Church of St. Agnes in Rome, two lambs are blessed and palliums are made from their wool. The pallium is a circle of woolen cloth decorated with crosses. It is worn about the neck and shoulders by the Catholic pope and archbishops.

35. Another famous
Christian martyr
who met death
during the persecution
under Diocletian
was a Christian soldier
named Sebastian.
His story is told here.

Another person martyred during the persecution under Diocletian was Sebastian, a soldier and a Christian. He often met Christians
who were in trouble during this period, and he
generously tried to help them as best he
could. A brave and able soldier, Sebastian was
promoted to posts of command.

In 303, when the persecution began, Sebastian was discharged from the army. Though
he had been born in Gaul and educated in
Milan, Sebastian moved to Rome and joined
the Christian community there. On the feast

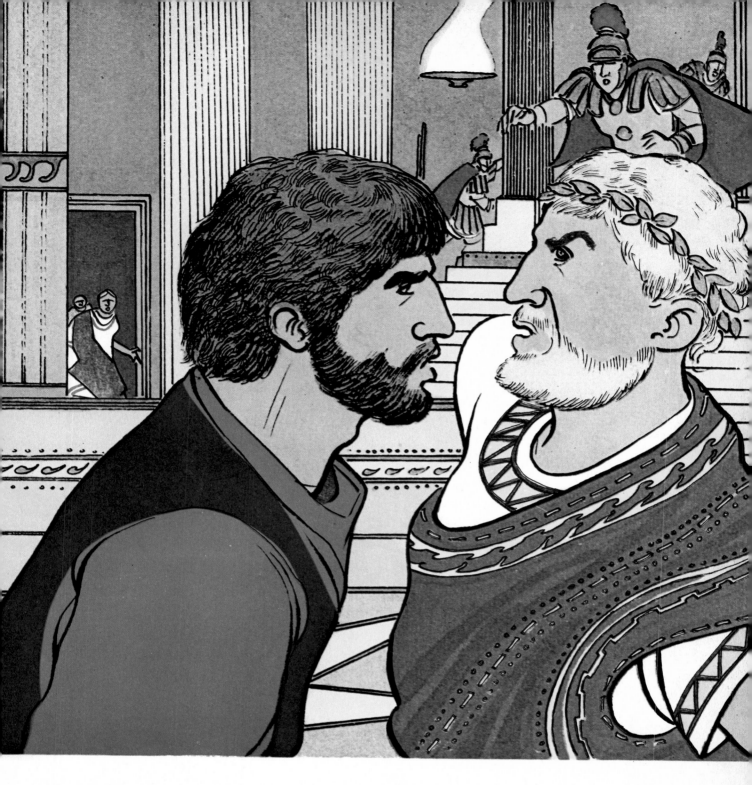

day of St. Peter and St. Paul, two of his Christian friends were killed while they prayed at the place where the two apostles were supposed to have been been martyred. Sebastian was greatly saddened. As time went on, many of his friends were killed, but still Sebastian encouraged other Christians to persevere in their faith.

On one occasion Sebastian himself was arrested and tied to a pillar. The story is told that soldiers shot arrows at him and left him for dead, bleeding from many wounds. But the mother of one of his friends saw that he was still breathing, took him home, and cared for him until he got better.

Legend tells us that some time after this, Sebastian met the emperor. He criticized the emperor for mistreating Christians. The emperor was furious and ordered that Sebastian be clubbed to death. Sebastian's corpse was then thrown into a sewer. But a Christian woman recovered his body and had it buried with honor in a catacomb.

36. Diocletian divided
the Roman empire
into an eastern and
a western section,
each with its own ruler.
This made the empire
easier to handle.
After Diocletian retired,
both Maxentius
and Constantine claimed
the western empire.

The burden of political and military tasks was too heavy for one emperor to handle. To solve this problem and to ensure peaceful succession to the imperial throne, Diocletian divided the empire into an eastern section and a western section. Each section would be ruled by an emperor, known as an Augustus, and each emperor would have an assistant, known as a Caesar. Diocletian was the emperor or Augustus in the East, assisted by Galerius. The emperor in the West was Maximian. His assistant was Constantius Chlorus. This system of rulership was known as a *tetrarchy,* because there were four rulers altogether.

Harmony and order prevailed while Diocletian ruled. No one seriously challenged his authority. The assistant Caesars mainly ruled over frontier areas and commanded the army. After more than twenty years of rule, Diocletian became ill and decided to retire to his palace in Split, in present-day Yugoslavia. He lived there another eight years. The emperor of the West, Maximian, retired at the same time. Their Caesars, Galerius and Constantius Chlorus, became the new emperors, or Augusti. They appointed two new Caesars to assist them.

One year later, however, Constantius Chlorus died. In Rome the son of Maximian, Maxentius, was elected emperor of the West. In Britain, however, the soldiers of Constantius Chlorus proclaimed his son, Constantine, emperor of the West. This eventually led to a bloody battle for the imperial throne.

During this politically troubled time, economic problems and heavy taxes made the situation worse in the western part of the empire. People living there became poorer as the economy declined. But agriculture and commerce continued to succeed in the eastern empire, especially in areas which were free of political turmoil.

37. Constantine went to Italy
with his army to fight
Maxentius for the throne.
Constantine was not
a Christian, but
he was told in a dream
to put the sign of Christ
on his soldiers' shields.
He did so, and won
the battle. He believed
that the Christian God
had helped him.

The struggle for power within the empire went on for years. More than one person claimed the imperial throne, and those who wanted to be emperor fought each other savagely.

One of those claiming the throne was Constantine, the son of Constantius Chlorus. His soldiers had proclaimed him emperor. Constantine was an energetic leader who loved power and he was a successful military commander. Later events would show that he was also a good administrator and lawmaker.

It seems that Constantine gave some thought to religion. He came from a class of pagans who scorned Christianity. As a young man and a soldier, he believed in many gods and chose to worship the god whose symbol was the sun. Gradually, he gave up this devotion and came to believe that there was only one God, but he did not believe in the Christian God.

In 312, Constantine was in Gaul with his army. He decided to go into Italy and fight his rival, Maxentius, who ruled Italy and Africa. Maxentius was thought to be much more powerful than Constantine, but the surprise invasion caught him unprepared. Constantine won northern Italy and marched toward Rome. There Maxentius gathered with his army and waited to do battle.

Constantine's war was not for the Christian religion. He was fighting for a throne. But something happened at this time to make him take a definite step toward Christianity. We do not know exactly what happened, but years later he told the church historian, Eusebius, that on the night before the battle with Maxentius, he had a vision. In the vision, he was told to put the sign of Christ—the first two letters of Christ's name in Greek—on his soldiers' shields. "In this sign you will conquer," the vision told him.

On October 28, 312, Constantine fought Maxentius at the Milvian Bridge, near Rome. Constantine won the battle, and he seemed to think that he owed his victory to the God of the Christians. Though not yet a Christian himself, Constantine now had the sign of Christ put on all his soldiers' uniforms and weapons. He also began to act in a helpful way toward Christians.

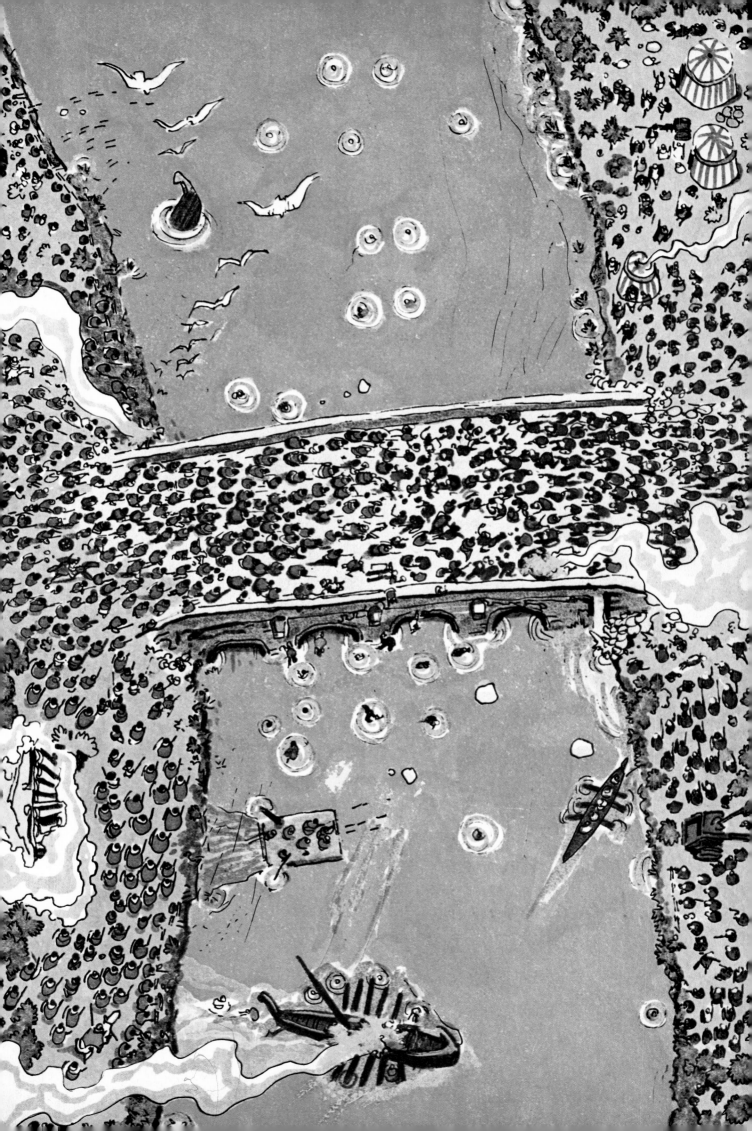

38. In 313, Constantine and Licinius—the eastern emperor—proclaimed the Edict of Milan, saying that Christians could follow their religion freely and would no longer be persecuted.

In 324, Constantine became emperor of both the East and the West. He built a new capital city—Constantinople. Today this city is called Istanbul.

With the defeat of Maxentius, Constantine became the sole master of the western part of the empire. In the East, Constantine's ally, Licinius, defeated his rivals and became chief ruler. In February 313, Constantine and Licinius met in Milan to decide the status of Christianity.

Their famous Edict of Milan recognized Christianity as a legal religion. This continued the policy set up by the dying Galerius in 311. It allowed Christians to profess their faith freely and restored confiscated properties to individuals and local churches.

Soon Constantine began to favor the Christian religion. Shortly after his victory over Maxentius, Constantine publicly admitted that he believed in the God of the Christians. Although Constantine was not baptized until

just before his death, he was a catechumen, a person learning about the Christian faith.

Licinius was not in favor of Christianity, and he began to persecute Christians in the East in 323. Constantine soon defeated Licinius. Then all power, authority, and honor was centered in Constantine, and he expressed his Christian convictions more openly. He surrounded himself with Christian advisers. He urged people to convert to Christianity, but he also declared that both the Christian and pagan religions were legally equal.

Constantine forbade the offering of sacrifices in honor of the emperor. The emperor was to be regarded as the servant of God on earth rather than as a god. This meant the emperor was to be obeyed and honored. Church and State were to work together, although Constantine felt he was master of the Church, just as the pagan emperors had been masters of the old pagan religion.

To complete the work of restoring the Roman empire, Constantine had a new capital city built on the strait of Bosporus. It was far to the east of Rome, between the Mediterranean Sea and the Black Sea. This city, called Constantinople, was clearly a Christian capital. It soon became wealthy and powerful. Power in the Roman empire had shifted eastward. The new capital ruled an empire that would last for more than a thousand years before falling to the Turks. This empire is usually called the Byzantine empire, because the city of Constantinople was built on the site of the ancient town of Byzantium. Today, Constantinople is called Istanbul, in Turkey.

39. Lactantius, a famous
pagan teacher, was
inspired by the example
of the Christian martyrs
during the persecution
by Diocletian.
He became a Christian
in 310. Lactantius
wanted to rewrite
pagan religious hymns
to honor the one true God.

During this time a Christian writer and teacher named Lactantius was highly esteemed by Constantine. Lucius Caecilius Firmianus Lactantius was born in Africa around the year 250. He grew up as a pagan, received a good education, and became a teacher of rhetoric. He and his teacher Arnobius were among the finest examples of cultured Latin pagans. Around 310, Arnobius became a Christian, and Lactantius followed his teacher's lead.

Lactantius did not get rid of the books and writings he had loved as a pagan. He thought, for example, that hymns to the pagan gods should be rewritten to praise the one true God. But conversion to Christianity did completely change his view of human history and its meaning. After living through the terrible persecution of Diocletian, he could not help but wonder at the survival and victory of the Church. Lactantius thought that God clearly had some hand in the course of human history. Christ would never abandon human beings, nor would he always require the Church to endure persecutions. Lactantius saw the death of the persecutors as a sign of God's love for the Church.

Lactantius felt that pagan philosophers could not speak with authority about God because they failed to recognize God's Son. Truth and eternal life came only from Jesus, who revealed the true meaning of human existence.

40. Around 318-319, Arius,
a parish priest
in Alexandria, Egypt,
began to preach
a mistaken belief
about Jesus.
The Church decided
that Arius was wrong.
But his teaching,
called Arianism,
continued to spread.

Under Constantine's rule, Christians were safe from persecution and could reflect on the meaning of their faith. They were particularly fascinated by the figure of Jesus. They wanted to know exactly who he was and what he had to say to human beings. Different views—some of them seriously wrong, according to the Church—arose.

One such erroneous view was that of Arius. Born in Libya and educated in Egypt, he became a parish priest in Alexandria. He led an ascetic life, denying himself comforts. He was a great preacher and had the ability to express himself well and convincingly.

Around 318-319, Arius began to teach an erroneous view: that Jesus was not God but a special, unique being created by God. Jesus was something like God, except that he could weep and suffer, whereas God could not. Jesus was also something like a human being, said Arius, but he did not have a human soul.

Arius's view attracted many followers, including theologians, clergy, and lay people of the East. They thought it made sense, and they found it fairly easy to understand.

Many other Christians, however, quickly opposed the teaching of Arius. They were convinced that if Jesus was not truly God, then there was no way for human beings to be saved or to make contact with the divine. The bishop of Alexandria argued with Arius. He praised Arius for his efforts to explore Christian doctrine, but said that Arius was mistaken and that he had to abandon his view. But Arius still refused to obey the bishop. He continued to try to convince others that his idea about Jesus was correct, and he found supporters in Alexandria and in other parts of the eastern empire.

In 319, the bishops of Egypt then held a meeting called a synod. About one hundred bishops came to the synod to discuss Arius's teachings. Arius spoke eloquently, explaining his religious beliefs. The bishops then reached a conclusion: Arius and fourteen of his followers were to be expelled from the Church for their wrong view, which was called heresy. Arius had to give up his parish or give up his beliefs.

Arius withdrew to Nicomedia, a large city in the eastern empire. The bishop of that city, Eusebius, supported Arius, and the city became the center of Arianism. The theological argument went on and continued to spread, greatly disturbing peace between Christians.

41. Athanasius spoke out
strongly against Arianism.
Athanasius was dedicated
to the Church's service
and worked hard
for church unity.
As bishop of Alexandria
he wrote many works
explaining the truths
of the Christian faith.

Athanasius was a great opponent of Arianism. He fought against it all his life, putting up with hardships and showing his ardent love for Church unity.

Athanasius was born into a Christian family of Alexandria in 295. As a young child, he lived through the terrible ordeal of Diocletian's persecution. Instead of driving him away from Christianity, the persecution strengthened Athanasius's character and his faith.

As a young man, Athanasius came to know Antony, the founder of Christian monasticism in the Egyptian desert. Athanasius never forgot the great saint. Later he wrote a famous biography of St. Antony, which brought the ideals of monasticism to the West.

Athanasius received his Christian religious education in the theological school of Alexandria in which Clement and Origen had taught. There he came to know teachers who were earnest seekers of the truth. In fact, in the past some teachers of the school had died during the persecution by Diocletian. Athanasius sincerely desired to seek the truth and defend it. Rather than becoming a philosopher or a thinker, Athanasius dedicated himself to the Church. He wanted the truth of the Church to prevail, and later he was willing to use power and a network of plans to achieve that goal.

Athanasius became a deacon in the Church. Later he was secretary to the bishop of Alexandria at the time Arius began to preach the doctrine of Arianism. Athanasius had no doubts about the matter. He believed that Jesus Christ was both true God and true human being. Jesus was one with God in a basic, essential way. God and Jesus could not be separated from each other. The powers of God had become incarnate in the man named Jesus. If Christ were not God, said Athanasius, Christ could not have brought salvation to human beings, and human beings would have no hope of salvation except through their own moral effort. But since Christ was both God and man, human beings could look to him for salvation. And this salvation was found only in the life of the Church, which was a mysterious continuation of the life of Jesus. It could not be found in mere human activity.

Athanasius never stopped defending these strong convictions in his writings and teaching. He was particularly active after 328, when he became the bishop of Alexandria.

42. Arguments over Arianism
seemed about to divide
the Church.
Emperor Constantine
called the bishops
together in council
at Nicaea to talk about
the doctrine.
The bishops decided
that Arianism was wrong.
They said that Jesus was
"true God of true God,
begotten, not made."

The debate between the Arians and their opponents grew more and more serious. It threatened to divide the Church completely and to start a real civil war in the empire. Constantine believed that defending church unity was part of his God-given mission as emperor. Following the advice of his theological adviser, Bishop Hosius of Cordova, Constantine ordered a church council to meet in Nicaea, near Constantinople, where the emperor often spent his vacations. It was to be an ecumenical council, including bishops from the Church around the world.

More than 300 bishops attended this council. Almost all the bishops from the Greek-speaking East came, as well as about fifteen from the Latin-speaking West. The group was too large for the church of Nicaea, and so Constantine let them use his imperial palace.

The council was inaugurated solemnly on May 20, 325, by Constantine himself. In his opening speech, he urged the bishops to seek peace and inner harmony within the Church.

The debate grew lively as the Arians presented their ideas about Christ. The majority of the bishops did not agree with the Arians.

So the bishops tried to agree on a statement that would properly express the true belief of the Christian Church. They affirmed that Jesus Christ was of the same substance as the Father. In other words, he was God just as the Father was God; he was not a created being. Jesus, the Council said, had been begotten by the Father before creation began.

Today the Creed still uses the phrases set forth by the Council of Nicaea about Jesus: "God from God, Light from Light, true God from true God, begotten, not made, one in Being with the Father."

The bishops reached a shared opinion on all the other major points. The Council, which had been called because of the danger of deep division within the Church, confirmed the Church's unity.

For some time even the Arians did not dare to attack the Council of Nicaea openly. For what Constantine said seemed true: "What has been decided by three hundred bishops is nothing else but the will of God, since the Holy Spirit present in those men made clear to them the will of God himself."

43. Constantius, the emperor after Constantine, liked Arianism, but Hosius and Athanasius worked together to defend the Church against Arianism.

get rid of their fierce opponent, Athanasius. They succeeded in getting him removed from his office and exiled by Constantine. In 328 the post of church adviser to the emperor was taken over by Eusebius of Nicomedia. He liked Arianism and tried to influence Constantine toward that view.

When Constantine died in 337, the situation grew worse for the Church. Constantius, Constantine's son, became sole emperor in

Another churchman besides Athanasius stood by the Church during those difficult years. This was Hosius, the bishop of Cordova, Spain. He was born around 260 and lived to be 99 years old.

Bishop Hosius had the difficult role of adviser to Emperor Constantine. He did much useful work for the Church in this role, helping the emperor to understand and support the Church position. Hosius favored the summoning of the Council of Nicaea, at which he also represented the pope. He, like Athanasius, was a strong champion of the view of Jesus which was affirmed at the Council of Nicaea.

After the Council, the Arians continued to defend and promote Arianism. In Alexandria, where they had some strength, they tried to

351. He showed clearly that he liked Arianism. Also, he wanted the Church to be a State Church, controlled by the emperor.

Hosius and Athanasius continued to be the two great defenders of the Church. Athanasius returned from exile, and a strong friendship grew up between the two men. When Athanasius was driven into exile a second time, Hosius offered him support and encouragement.

The emperor continued to interfere in church affairs. He felt that he had the right to control the Church, just as Constantine had done. In 355, Hosius strongly criticized Emperor Constantius for his actions. Hosius told the emperor that men of the Church should not govern earthly kingdoms and that emperors should not offer sacrifices to God. Hosius's defense of the Church and his support of Athanasius later led to his own exile.

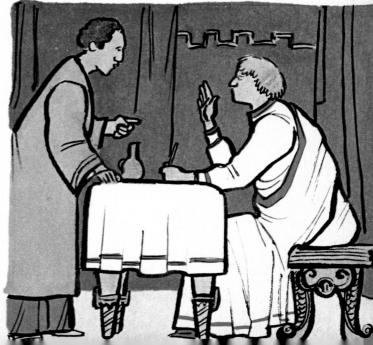

44. Eusebius, bishop
of Caesarea in Palestine,
was a famous writer
and speaker. He wrote a
history of the Church
which told the story
of the Church
from the beginning
until the year 324.
Eusebius admired
Constantine very much.

Another man, who lived about the same time as Hosius, wrote a history of the Church from its beginnings and recounted the life and deeds of Constantine. This was Eusebius of Caesarea. (He should not be taken for bishop Eusebius of Nicomedia.)

Eusebius was born in Caesarea (Palestine) around 263. The city had been a center of Christian study ever since Origen had founded a famous school there. Like Origen, a priest named Pamphilus started his own Christian school in Caesarea. Eusebius attended this school, and Pamphilus became his teacher, friend, and spiritual adviser.

During the persecution by Diocletian, Pamphilus suffered martyrdom. Eusebius escaped to the Egyptian desert. After the Edict of Milan allowed Christians to worship openly again, Eusebius returned to Caesarea, where he was elected bishop. During the debate over Arianism and the Council of Nicaea, Eusebius tried to bring the two sides together.

Eusebius of Caesarea admired Constantine greatly. He never forgot that Constantine had established peace between the empire and the Church after centuries of persecution. On the twentieth and thirtieth anniversaries of Constantine's rise to the imperial throne,

Eusebius praised him highly in public speeches. Eusebius also dedicated a funeral eulogy to Constantine after his death.

Eusebius wrote a huge number of works. By far his most important work was his *History of the Church*. In it he told the story of the Church from the very beginning to the year 324. It was a work of great importance, and Eusebius is often called the father of church history. He also wrote a life of Constantine, in which he lavished praise on the emperor for his deeds.

**45. Though the Church
had problems,
it now grew freely,
without fear of being
persecuted. New churches
were built, bishops
became important
in public life,
and more and more people
became Christian.**

For those alive in Constantine's day, his rule marked a big change in the life of the Church. This is how Eusebius described it: "People were freed from all the fear that had weighed down on them before. They began to celebrate great feasts and hold joyous gatherings. Light lit up their lives. . . . Dance and song in city and countryside gave honor, first to God, the king of kings, for that is what they had been taught, and then to the goodly emperor and his children beloved by God."

Now the Church came to new life in the empire. Churches were built everywhere, some of them sponsored by the emperor himself. In Palestine, Asia Minor, Rome, and the West many basilicas were built during the reign of Constantine. These new buildings were often huge and elaborate, and Byzantine art was developed to decorate them.

Christian bishops were welcomed at the imperial court and they were treated with great respect. Bishops were now considered to be on the same high level as Roman senators and patricians. Soon bishops were allowed to act as judges, even in cases that were not church matters.

The work of spreading the Christian faith was most important. Within the space of one century, from 300 to 400, Christianity became the religion of the majority within the empire. Every Christian community took part in this work, led by local bishops and the monks who were now beginning to appear in the East. New groups of Christians were organized as local churches under the direction of a bishop. As the cities and the surrounding countryside became more Christian, preachers and missionaries went to more remote rural places to spread the Gospel. Following ancient custom, the clergy and bishops were most

often nominated by the whole community. Lay people usually showed their approval by giving a loud shout.

This expansion created some new problems. During the times of persecution, only truly converted people had entered the Christian churches. Now many people became Christians only because the emperor favored Christianity or because everyone seemed to be doing it. To answer this problem, the Church began to give more care and attention to the education of new Christians. The Church also showed greater concern for renewal in liturgy and the use of the sacraments.

46. Christianity was now a religion with special privileges.
Emperor Constantius tried to force pagans to become Christian.
Some Christians now began to use violence against pagans, but the church authorities defended pagans and reminded their people that true conversions were made freely.

The Edict of Milan in 313 granted freedom of worship to all, so that even Christians could profess their faith openly. But Christianity soon changed from being just another approved religion to being a religion with special privileges. Constantine favored the Church, helped it in many ways, and respected its leaders. But he always refused to make laws against non-Christians and he was baptized only on his deathbed.

Constantine's sons gave up the policy of religious freedom for all. They acted against the old pagan religion. In 341, Constantine's son, emperor Constantius, forbade all pagan sacrifices. A few years later he ordered the closing of all pagan temples. Pagans who refused to obey the edicts would lose their property and might even be put to death. Thus the emperor used the power of the government to force Christianity on people.

The emperor's actions encouraged some Christians to use force and violence against pagans. They destroyed pagan statues, took away pagans' property, and vandalized pagan temples.

The majority of Christians felt that no one should be forced to adopt a certain religion. The church authorities constantly reminded Christians that the only true conversions were those made freely by people.

Another change took place at this time. During the time of persecution, the Church had had to stress its originality and its unusual message. The Church had also had to show that it had something to contribute to human beings. Now the Church looked for what was good in pagan culture and tried to save it from destruction. Some Christians insisted that paganism had nothing to contribute to Christian life. Fortunately, the view of those hostile Christians did not win out, and much pagan learning was preserved by Christian scholars and teachers.

47. The great power
of the Roman Emperor
became a danger
to the Church
at this time.
Emperor Constantius
tried to interfere
with church affairs.
Constantius liked
Arianism, and he wanted
the bishops to condemn
Athanasius, who defended
Christian truth.

Constantine was a very strong-willed ruler. He thought that the emperor had a very special position with respect to the Church. Constantine believed that a Christian emperor was not only the protector of the Church but was also a kind of universal bishop with full power over the Church. Thus the emperor stood above all, even the Church's bishops, on all matters. He was even in charge of church worship and the teaching of the Gospel message. These ideas could cause serious problems if an emperor had unusual views of his own regarding doctrine or some other part of church life.

The emperor Constantius was to be such a ruler. In 342, a synod met in Sardica, which today is Sofia in Bulgaria. At this synod two of Constantius's representatives defended a heretical point of view—that is, a religious belief different from the standard Christian belief. The bishops at the synod refused to accept the heretical belief, and some of their decisions criticized Constantius's religious policy. The emperor answered by exiling certain priests and bishops.

After the death of his brother Constans in 350, Constantius became emperor of both the

eastern and western empires. He tried to control the Church even more. At a council in Milan in 355, Constantius asked the council to condemn Athanasius. Constantius did this because he liked Arianism, while Athanasius defended the orthodox or standard Christian view and actively opposed Arianism.

To get what he wanted, Constantius even hid and listened in secret to what the bishops were saying. The bishops reacted strongly against the emperor and his tactics. Constantius, in turn, demanded: "What I wish should be the law of the Church."

Constantius exiled many bishops who opposed him, and he mistreated the envoys of the pope. He even sent Pope Liberius into exile. But in the end, Constantius did not succeed in controlling the Church. Upon his death, the exiled bishops returned home amid rejoicing.

48. In 360, Julian became
   emperor of the West.
   He had given up
   his Christian faith
   and become a pagan.
   As emperor,
   he tried to bring back
   the pagan religion.
   But he failed and died
   after ruling two years.

In February 360, the Roman soldiers in Gaul proclaimed their leader, Julian, emperor. Julian is known in history as the man who tried but failed to bring back paganism as the religion of the Roman empire. Julian had been brought up as a Christian, and so he is called Julian the Apostate. (An apostate is a person who turns against his or her religious faith.)

Julian was born in 330. He was a nephew of Constantine. When Constantius became emperor, Julian's father and brother were killed. Julian was raised as a Christian, but he had no strong Christian teachers to help him learn and thus love the Gospel. He blamed his cousin, the Christian emperor Constantius, for the murder of his father and brother. Julian studied pagan philosophers and he went to Athens to see where Greek culture had begun. Later, he took part in the pagan religious rites of Mithra.

In 355 Julian was summoned from his study and appointed Caesar, the emperor's chief helper. He was sent to Gaul. To the surprise of many people, Julian was a fine army commander and he was very popular with his soldiers. His rule was fair and beneficial.

In 360 Constantius ordered Julian to send

Roman soldiers to help out in a war against the Persians in the East. The soldiers rebelled against Constantius and proclaimed Julian Augustus. Soon after that, Constantius died. On his deathbed, he declared Julian his successor.

Emperor Julian openly renounced Christianity and began to encourage all the old forms of pagan religion. He restored all the old privileges to the pagan religion and took away the privileges of Christians. He removed Christians from public office. He also forbade Christians to teach the ancient classics, probably to make Christians go to

pagan schools for higher learning. He encouraged erroneous doctrines within the Church, and he made plans to rebuild the Jewish temple in Jerusalem. Julian did not favor open persecution of the Church, but it is clear that he wanted to destroy Christianity by strengthening the pagan religion and Judaism.

Julian's rule lasted only two years. In 363, he died in a military campaign, and his work of restoring paganism died also. The old religion had lost its last chance for revival.

49. Pope Liberius, though
weak in some ways,
helped unify the Church
by his support
of the bishops
and by his letters.
He upheld the creed
or statement of beliefs
written at the
Council of Nicaea.

During the reign of Emperor Constantius II, nine years before Julian became emperor, Liberius was chosen pope of Rome. He followed the standard or orthodox Christian beliefs set forth in the Nicene Creed. But Constantius tried to make Liberius become an Arian, as Constantius himself was.

Constantius also wished to put an end to Athanasius of Alexandria's defense of the Christian faith. He charged Athanasius with being a rebel, and wanted Liberius to agree that Athanasius should be condemned. When Liberius refused to do this, Contantius had the pope exiled.

Almost three years later, Liberius gave in to the emperor's threats and signed a statement saying that he agreed with Arian beliefs.

Liberius was allowed to come back to Rome, and people demanded that he be reinstated as bishop.

Even though Liberius had been forced to say that he was an Arian, he still believed in the true Christian faith. After the death of Constantius in 360, he tried to bring unity between those Christians who upheld the Nicene Creed and those who disagreed with it. Liberius also tried to strengthen the authority of the pope of Rome.

In 364, Valens was emperor in the East. He was an Arian, and he exiled some bishops who preached against Arianism.

A large group of eastern bishops chose three representatives to go to Rome and ask the Christian emperor of the West and

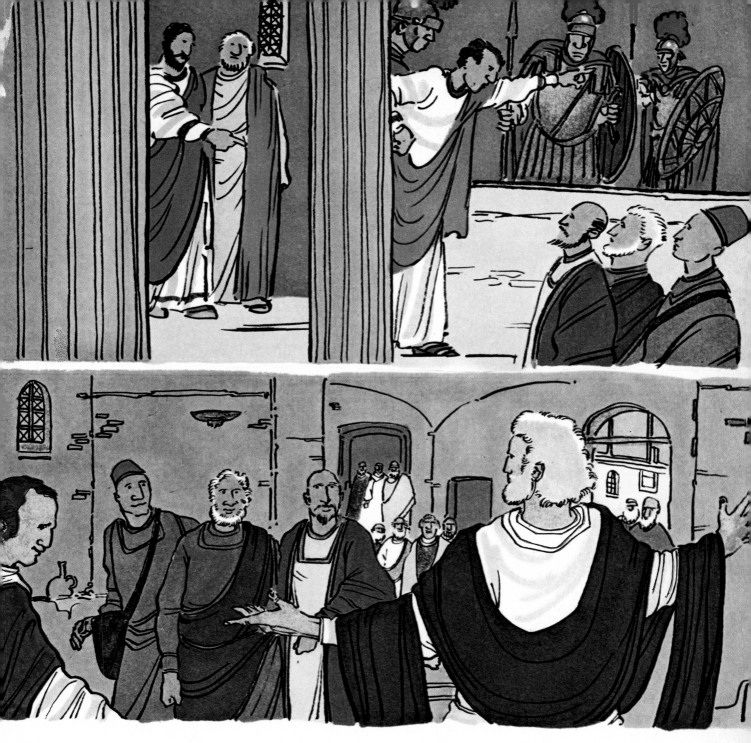

the pope for help. When the three bishops arrived in Rome, the emperor was away. Pope Liberius met with them, and he gave them all the help he could. Also, he encouraged and directed them to believe and teach the Nicene Creed, as written at the Council of Nicaea, and to give up false beliefs.

The pope wrote letters to all the eastern bishops who believed in the true faith, telling them the same thing. These letters were taken back to the East by the three bishops. At the pope's request, bishops of Gaul, North Africa, and Italy wrote to the eastern bishops, professing their faith in the Nicene Creed. In this way, the unity of the true faith was proclaimed, and Pope Liberius made up to some extent for his earlier weakness and error.

50. The work of spreading the Gospel of Christ continued in town and country areas. One of the greatest missionary bishops was Martin of Tours.

The Church continued to work for the conversion of people to Christianity and the growth of mission areas. Around 350, missionary work moved out from the towns into the country areas. In Gaul, Martin of Tours did much to spread the Gospel message to the surrounding countryside.

Martin was born in present-day Hungary. The son of an officer in the Roman army, he himself became a soldier for a time. A famous legend tells that he once gave half his cloak to a poor beggar. Later he saw the beggar in a dream and realized that the beggar had been Christ.

Martin was still a catechumen at the time of this legendary event. He was baptized around the age of eighteen and became a hermit on an island near Genoa in what is now Italy.

Around 371 Martin returned to Gaul and became a monk. Disciples gathered around him, but soon he was elected bishop of Tours.

He continued to lead a deeply religious life and to promoted monasticism in Gaul. But Martin also resolved to convert the pagan people living in the country areas of his see or diocese. Many of them were Celts who still followed their ancient tribal customs. They offered sacrifices, venerated trees and water sites as sacred places, and built small sanctuaries for worship and prayer. These pagans held on to their traditions loyally, but Martin preached the Gospel with energy and enthusiasm. Sometimes he may have been too vigorous, destroying pagan sanctuaries to show that the Christian God was more powerful than other deities.

Martin converted many pagans to Christianity in what is now called France. In every area where he preached, Martin built and left behind a chapel or a small group of monks to continue the work of spreading the Gospel message.

Martin's way of life is just one of the outstanding examples set by many people in the Church during this period. Many dedicated Christians set out from towns and villages to convert people in the surrounding countryside who had not yet heard about Christianity. At about the same time Martin preached in France, St. Victricio of Rouen did this kind of work in Flanders; in Italy, St. Virgil of Trent worked in the Alpine region.

51. Around the year 280, some
Christians in Egypt
and in Syria gave up
their jobs and their
family life. They went
to desert places
to spend their lives
in prayer. They lived
in poverty, suffering
hardships so that they
could be like Jesus.
This was the beginning
of Christian monasticism.

Around the year 280, individual Christians in Egypt and eastern Syria began to give up the community life they had been living. They gave up their work, their chances for careers and economic success, and the comforts of home in order to lead lives of complete poverty in lonely areas. This was the beginning of Christian monasticism. Monasticism was a way of life in which people promised to live in poverty, unmarried, and obedient to a leader. People who lived a monastic life were called monks.

Monks who lived by themselves were called anchorites. (The word *anchorite* comes from a Greek work meaning "withdraw.") In a few decades, there were many anchorites living in small huts or in rocky caves. Some stayed by themselves all the time. Others would meet from time to time to seek advice from one particular person who was their spiritual adviser. We do not know who the very first anchorites were; but one of the first great monks was Antony, whose story is told in the next chapter.

The basic motive behind this new and hard way of life was a desire to imitate Jesus. Monks wanted to devote themselves entirely to God and to carry a cross as Jesus had done. They knew that martyrdom was one noble way to imitate Jesus, and so they tried to endure the sufferings and hardships of their everyday lives as a kind of martyrdom. They dedicated themselves to poverty and virginity. This meant that they gave up wordly goods and the possibility of family life.

Monks wanted to follow Jesus' advice: "If you would be perfect, go, sell what you possess and give to the poor, and you will have treasure in heaven; and come, follow me" (Matthew 19:21).

Monasticism spread rapidly in the East, and it would eventually have a great impact on the West as well. It still survives today as an important part of the heritage and life of the Church.

52. Antony of Egypt
was a famous monk
of this time.
Other people went
to live in the desert
as he did, and Antony
shared his wisdom
with them.
Each monk lived alone,
withdrawn from the world.

The most famous monk of this early monastic period was St. Antony. He lived a long life, from around 251 to around 356.

When he was around the age of twenty, this young Egyptian listened to the Gospel passage in which Jesus advised the rich young man to give up all his worldly goods and come follow him. Antony felt that this advice was spoken to him personally. He gave part of his possessions to his sister and sold the rest to give the money to people in need. His sister was younger than he, so he put her under the care of some good people. Then Antony withdrew to a lonely place far away from the city. He devoted himself to manual labor and to prayer, attaching special importance to reading Holy Scripture.

Monks, like other human beings, must face temptations. Antony was no exception. The stories about him tell of his long struggles with the devil, who tempted Antony to turn people away from God.

After spending a long time in the desert, Antony went to help the persecuted Christians of Alexandria. To them he seemed to be a person filled with God who had just come from a sacred place. Antony wanted to be a martyr for Christ, but God had other plans. Other people wanted to join Antony as hermits, prayerful monks of the desert area. He returned to the desert with these new monks. They called Antony *Abbas*, which means "father," because he was their guide and counselor. From him they learned how to develop the spiritual strength to overcome temptations and grow in perfect love for God. They were called *anchorites* because each monk lived alone, withdrawn from the world.

Around 313 Antony tried to withdraw farther into the desert to be by himself. Again others came to visit him for advice and help. His life of prayer had given him deep wisdom, and he shared this with other monks.

53. Pachomius of Thebes began another kind of monastic life. Instead of living alone, the monks lived together as a community in a big house.

Monastic life today is usually different from the kind of life Antony lived. Antony and his monks lived for the most part in isolated areas by themselves, using grottoes or caves for shelter. Only now and then would they come together for prayer and meetings. Today monks usually live in large houses called monasteries, where they pray, study, and work together. The founder of this kind of monasticism was Pachomius, another Egyptian.

Pachomius was born a pagan in Thebes around 287. When he was about twenty-three, he was drafted into the Roman army, as many young men of his day were. In Thebes he met people known as Christians. They tried to help and cheer up the new soldiers before they set off for foreign places. Inspired by them, Pachomius decided that he would become a Christian and help other people if he managed to leave military service alive.

Pachomius, much to his surprise, was soon released from military service. Remembering his promise, he took instruction and was baptized. After three years, he withdrew to the desert to live the life of a monk. For some years he lived alone, as monks usually did. Now and then he visited a famous monk named Palemon to get advice and spiritual help. Gradually Pachomius came to feel that living alone was not the right kind of life for him. The story is told that in a dream an angel told Pachomius that God wanted him to reconcile other people with God and bring them closer to God.

Pachomius decided to build a big house. He would take in all those who desired to live with him as monks. Thus began the first community of men who vowed to live together in order to pray and fully obey the will of God. These men were called *cenobites.* The word comes from two Greek words meaning "common life." These monks lived in community, sharing a common way of life.

54. Many people joined
Pachomius's monastery,
and soon many more
houses had to be built.
The monks worked
to support the community.
Some baked bread
and cooked food,
some herded sheep
or caught fish.
All did some work, and
an important idea
in their lives was that
they should help others
at all times.
Reading the Bible
gave the monks guidance
in this new way of life.

Many persons soon joined Pachomius in the house he had built. New arrivals were asked to give up all their possessions and to live with the other members as if all had one heart and one soul. Praying together and helping each other, the monks tried to love God deeply and share his love with others.

Soon Pachomius's house in Tabennae, on the banks of the Nile River, was too small to hold all the members of the community. Pachomius and his monks built eight more houses while Pachomius himself was still alive. Women, too, wanted to follow this new way of life. These women included Pachomius's own sister. Houses were built for them as well.

Life in each of Pachomius's houses was carefully arranged. The monastery land was

surrounded by a wall to separate it from the world. To enter the monastery, one had to go through the doorkeeper's lodge. In the center of the monastery was a big hall. This was a common area—that is, it was for all the monks to use. The monks gathered in this hall to celebrate various functions together. The dining room was also a common room.

The monastery was divided into various buildings. About thirty or forty monks lived in each building under the direction of a superior and an assistant superior. Each monk had certain duties to perform for the benefit of the community, including working with his hands.

A monk might be a baker, a shepherd, or a fisherman. By selling their wares and cultivating the soil, the monks could take care of their basic needs. Thus a few hundred monks lived together in a holy community.

Pachomius often told his monks that they should help each other at all times. This theme guided their life together. In the Bible the monks found strength to follow this new way of life. Pachomius wanted them to learn many passages of the Bible by heart, and so all the monks had to learn how to read. Like members of a family, his monks were to take care of each other as well as themselves.

55. Basil was well-educated, wealthy, and seemed about to begin a brilliant career.
In 356, he gave up everything to become a monk. He lived alone at first, but other monks joined him.
Basil's monks were much like Pachomius's, but they gave more attention to reading the Bible and other sacred writings.

In the last part of the fourth century, Basil the Great did much to spread Christianity. He was greatly talented as a thinker, organizer, and reformer.

Basil was born around 330 in Caesarea, Cappadocia, a part of what is now called Turkey. He came from a noble family that was very loyal to the Church. His mother, Emilia, was the daughter of a Christian martyr. His father was a famous Christian orator. Two of Basil's brothers, Gregory and Peter, later became bishops and saints; his older sister Macrina became famous as a nun and a reformer of monasteries.

After learning the basics from his father, Basil went to school in his native city. Then he went to Constantinople, the capital of the empire, to learn from famous teachers there. Around the age of twenty he went to Athens, Greece. There he became friends with Gregory of Nanzianzus, a young man with great writing talent who also came from Cappadocia. This friendship was important. Basil was a fine thinker and organizer. Gregory of Nanzianzus was a fine speaker and writer. Gregory, Basil's younger brother, was also a great thinker. These three men would have an important influence on the Church of their day. They would also contribute much thought to the development of Christian doctrine. Even today their thinking about the Trinity—Father, Son, and Holy Spirit—is an important part of church belief.

In 356 Basil returned home. Wealthy, educated, and self-confident, he had a brilliant career ahead of him. But suddenly he changed his mind. He later described it this way: "Suddenly one day, like someone coming out of a deep sleep, I opened my eyes to the wonderful light of the Gospel truth and saw the uselessness of this world's wisdom."

Basil gave away his inheritance to the poor and went off alone to live the life of a monk. Soon he was joined by other companions. Using his great organizing ability, Basil soon founded many monasteries. He wrote two rules, or ways of life, for these monasteries. Monasteries based on his rules came to be called Basilian. His monasteries were much like those of Pachomius, but his rule gave greater attention to the study of Sacred Scripture and other Christian writings.

56. Basil became bishop
of Caesarea in 370.
He supported the Church
against Arianism,
and he urged rich people
to help the poor.
He taught that wealth
is given to people
by God so that they can
use it to help others.

Basil had left the world to live the life of a monk, but his work of founding and organizing monasteries soon made him famous. The bishop of Caesarea wanted Basil to be his assistant, and so he ordained Basil a priest. Gregory of Nanzianzus, Basil's close friend, wrote that Basil was a good adviser to his bishop, an able assistant, and a fine writer. At the time, many people still upheld Arian beliefs. Basil used his learning to convince people that Jesus Christ was truly God and truly man.

In 370 the bishop of Caesarea died. No one questioned who the next bishop should be. Basil was elected even though he did all he could to avoid being bishop. It was a difficult time for the Church because the Arians had managed to win the emperor over to their views. The emperor, Valens, wanted to convince the people that Arianism was right. He also wanted to win Basil over to that view. He sent his adviser, Modestus, to convince Basil that he should side with the emperor. Modestus first offered rewards to Basil. When that did not succeed, he threatened him.

Basil was quick to respond to Modestus and his threats. "Your threats do not frighten me. All you can do is kill me. But death is a victory for me because it will enable me to meet the Lord Jesus." Modestus was amazed by the courageous and noble words of Basil. He told him that no one had ever dared to speak to him so boldly. Basil replied: "Perhaps you have never had any dealings with a bishop. . . . When it comes to God and his business, we consider only him. Nothing else matters to us."

Basil did not just defend the truths of faith. He loved people deeply and did all he could to ease their sufferings. He gave away his own goods to the poor and he urged other wealthy people in the city to do the same. He told them that rich people were merely the stewards or caretakers of the wealth they had been granted by God. They were supposed to use their wealth to help the poor, not keep it for themselves like misers.

His example and preaching did not convince the rich to imitate him. So Basil established a hospital for sick people and the victims of epidemics. He also built an inn for people passing through the city who had no place to stay. He organized a kitchen to distribute food and meals to the needy as well. Anyone—Christian, Jew, or pagan—could find food at Basil's kitchen. For this reason Basil was much loved by all the people of his city.

57. Basil wrote a solemn lyrical form of the prayers used in the Liturgy of the Eucharist. This Basilian liturgy became the liturgy of the Russian Orthodox Church as well as of the Eastern Rite.

Christians of the Eastern Rite still use the Liturgy of St. Basil in their Mass. The basic elements of that Mass are the same as those of the Roman Rite, but Basil's rite is more solemn and poetic. At the beginning of the Mass, there is a procession. The priests and the deacon place the communion bread and wine beside the altar. Then come readings like those in the Mass of the Roman Rite. Next the real Basilian liturgy begins. It is a solemn eucharistic prayer, which Greek Christians call the anaphora and which Roman Catholics call the canon of the Mass.

The eucharistic prayer of Basil recalls the life and passion of Jesus. It asks God to change the bread and wine into the Body and Blood of Jesus, thus renewing the sacrifice that saved human beings from sin and punishment. Then a prayer to the Holy Spirit asks the Spirit to sanctify the offering and make it pleasing to God.

Long before Basil, of course, Christians had celebrated the eucharistic liturgy and composed prayers for it. But Basil increased and improved the prayers, thanks to his fine writing ability. In a short time the fame of his liturgy in Caesarea led Christians elsewhere to adopt it. It spread throughout the eastern Church. Around 800 it was translated into Old Slavonic by Saints Cyril and Methodius. In 987 it was introduced into Russia by the grand duke, Vladimir. There it became the liturgy of the whole Orthodox Church, as well as being the liturgy of the Eastern Rite of the Catholic Church.

When Basil died at around the age of fifty in 379, he had truly earned the title Basil the Great. The Church has kept that title for him ever since.

58. Emperor Theodosius encouraged the Church to hold a council to discuss the doctrine of the Trinity, but he did not interfere with church affairs. The eastern bishops assembled in Constantinople.

Seeking to understand their faith more clearly and deeply, Christians in the last part of the fourth century had to consider the nature of the Holy Spirit, and how the Holy Spirit was related to the Father and the Son.

Some Christians thought that the Holy Spirit was a creature, something like an angel but more powerful. The most ancient tradition of the Christian Church, however, held that the Holy Spirit was truly God.

The debate over this question was a very fierce one. The Arian emperor, Valens, took advantage of the split between Christians to advance his own religious policy.

Things changed when Theodosius came to the eastern imperial throne in 379. Theodosius had been a general in the region we today call Spain. He wanted all the Christians of the empire to follow the faith that had been handed down from the apostle Peter and proclaimed by the Roman Church. All should believe that the Father, Son, and Holy Spirit were equal in divinity and majesty, and that they formed a Holy Trinity.

In 381 about 150 bishops attended a church council held in Constantinople. It was not a council of the whole Church, but only of the eastern section of the Church. Its main purpose was to discuss problems affecting the eastern part of the Church. The conclusions of this council were so important that the whole Church accepted them.

At the opening of the council, Emperor Theodosius welcomed the bishops. But Theodosius did not invite the council to hold its sessions in his palace, nor did he take part in the council or send his own representatives, as Constantine had done at Nicaea. Thus the bishops were able to do their work in complete freedom.

The main topic of discussion at the council was the Holy Spirit. In the Gospels, Jesus told his disciples that he would send the Holy Spirit after he returned to his Father. The Holy Spirit would keep his disciples united and help them remain faithful to the faith he had taught them. Indeed, the Holy Spirit made it possible for all human beings to experience Jesus' presence after Jesus had died and risen from the dead. This being the case, said the Council of Constantinople, the Holy Spirit was not a created being, but was truly God. Furthermore, the bishops said that people who claimed that the Holy Spirit was only a creature were heretics.

1 *We believe in one God,*
the Father, the Almighty,
maker of heaven and earth,
of all that is seen and unseen.

2 *We believe in one Lord, Jesus Christ,*
the only Son of God, eternally begotten
of the Father, God from God,
Light from Light, true God from true God,
begotten, not made, one in Being
with the Father.
Through him all things were made.

59. The Council of Constantinople in 381 approved the Nicene Creed and added a section about the Holy Spirit. This is the same Creed many Christians pray today.

The council of Nicaea had met in 324 in Constantine's palace to heal divisions in the Church caused by the fight over Arianism. Followers of Arianism believed that Jesus was created by God but was not God. After discussing this issue, the Council of Nicaea agreed on a Creed which expressed the true belief of the Christian Church.

The Council of Constantinople in 381 accepted the Creed formulated by the Council of Nicaea. But it added a section to make it clear that the Holy Spirit was God. This Creed is the one recited by many Christians today at worship services.

3 *For us men and for our salvation*
he came down from heaven:
by the power of the Holy Spirit
he was born of the Virgin Mary,
and became man.

4 *For our sake he was crucified under*
Pontius Pilate;
he suffered, died, and was buried.

5 *On the third day he rose again in*
   fulfillment of the Scriptures;
he ascended into heaven
   and is seated at the right hand
      of the Father.

6 *He will come again in glory to judge the*
   living and the dead,
   and his kingdom will have no end.

7 *We believe in the Holy Spirit, the Lord,*
   the giver of life,
who proceeds from the Father and the Son.
With the Father and the Son he is
   worshiped and glorified.
   He has spoken through the Prophets.

8 *We believe in one holy catholic and*
   apostolic Church.

9 *We acknowledge one baptism for the*
   forgiveness of sins.

10 *We look for the resurrection of the dead,*
   and the life of the world to come.

Outline by Chapter

The Church Established

TERTULLIAN

CLEMENT

ORIGEN

Chapters   Dates

FABIAN

CYPRIAN

LAWRENCE

AGNES

SEBASTIAN

LACTANTIUS

Note to Readers: The *c.* before some dates is an abbreviation for *circa,* meaning "about" or "approximately."

ATHANASIUS

HOSIUS

EUSEBIUS

ANTONY

PACHOMIUS

BASIL